MW00941489

WHAT'S GOING ON?

Why I Believe We Are the
Rapture Generation

DR. ED KING

WESTBOW
PRESS®
A DIVISION OF THOMAS NELSON
& ZONDERVAN

Copyright © 2018 Dr. Ed King.

All rights reserved. No part of this book may be used or reproduced by any means, graphic, electronic, or mechanical, including photocopying, recording, taping or by any information storage retrieval system without the written permission of the author except in the case of brief quotations embodied in critical articles and reviews.

This book is a work of non-fiction. Unless otherwise noted, the author and the publisher make no explicit guarantees as to the accuracy of the information contained in this book and in some cases, names of people and places have been altered to protect their privacy.

WestBow Press books may be ordered through booksellers or by contacting:

WestBow Press
A Division of Thomas Nelson & Zondervan
1663 Liberty Drive
Bloomington, IN 47403
www.westbowpress.com
1 (866) 928-1240

Because of the dynamic nature of the Internet, any web addresses or links contained in this book may have changed since publication and may no longer be valid. The views expressed in this work are solely those of the author and do not necessarily reflect the views of the publisher, and the publisher hereby disclaims any responsibility for them.

Any people depicted in stock imagery provided by Getty Images are models, and such images are being used for illustrative purposes only. Certain stock imagery © Getty Images.

ISBN: 978-1-9736-3887-2 (sc)
ISBN: 978-1-9736-3886-5 (hc)
ISBN: 978-1-9736-3888-9 (e)

Library of Congress Control Number: 2018910632

Print information available on the last page.

WestBow Press rev. date: 01/10/2019

Unless otherwise cited, all scripture taken from the King James Version of the Bible.

Scripture taken from the New King James Version®. Copyright © 1982 by Thomas Nelson. Used by permission. All rights reserved.

Scripture quotations marked (TLB) are taken from The Living Bible copyright © 1971. Used by permission of Tyndale House Publishers, Inc., Carol Stream, Illinois 60188. All rights reserved.

Scripture quotations marked (NLT) are taken from the Holy Bible, New Living Translation, copyright ©1996, 2004, 2007, 2013, 2015 by Tyndale House Foundation. Used by permission of Tyndale House Publishers, Inc., Carol Stream, Illinois 60188. All rights reserved.

Scripture quotations marked MSG are taken from THE MESSAGE, copyright © 1993, 1994, 1995, 1996, 2000, 2001, 2002 by Eugene H. Peterson. Used by permission of NavPress. All rights reserved. Represented by Tyndale House Publishers, Inc.

Scripture quotations marked (NIV) are taken from the Holy Bible, New International Version®, NIV®. Copyright © 1973, 1978, 1984, 2011 by Biblica, Inc.™ Used by permission of Zondervan. All rights reserved worldwide. www.zondervan.com The "NIV" and "New International Version" are trademarks registered in the United States Patent and Trademark Office by Biblica, Inc.

Scripture taken from the American Standard Version of the Bible.

Scripture quotations taken from the Amplified® Bible (AMP), Copyright © 2015 by The Lockman Foundation Used by permission.

Scripture quotations taken from the Amplified® Bible (AMPC), Copyright © 1954, 1958, 1962, 1964, 1965, 1987 by The Lockman Foundation Used by permission.

Taken from the HOLY BIBLE: EASY-TO-READ VERSION © 2001 by World Bible Translation Center, Inc. and used by permission.

CONTENTS

DEDICATION

For her enduring love, tireless work—helping build our ministry into something meaningful and sustaining—and standing alongside me in my journey to know God more fully and accurately, I dedicate this book to my wife, Nora. Not only is she my much better half, but she is also the co-pastor of our church and a great woman of God who desires more than anything else to be the earthly representation of "the Proverbs 31 Woman."

I think she's nailed it.

INTRODUCTION

With all my heart, I believe that we are the rapture generation. Although no one knows the day and the hour of Jesus's return, I am confident it is imminent. Here is what the Bible says about it:

> However, no one knows the day or hour when these things will happen, not even the angels in heaven or the Son himself. Only the Father knows. (Mark 13:32 NLT)

The purpose of this book is to share solid biblical information with you to illustrate how the signs of the times are lining up for Jesus's return at the rapture. There are altogether too many signs appearing and circumstances playing out for it to be any other way.

If you visit your local Christian bookstore, you will find numerous books and study materials dedicated solely to the book of Revelation and the end times. In fact, I have many of them in my personal library. However, this book is different. It not only focuses on the biblical truths found in Revelation and other places, it also looks at how those realities affect us today.

Current events are shaping our future in dramatic ways, and Bible prophecy is on target and credible to life in today's world. That's why I believe that many of us will have the incredible opportunity to witness the second coming of the Lord Jesus Christ before we breathe our last.

Because I wrote this book for the day and hour we are living, you are going to read some things in the following chapters that are missing from other books about the end times. We are going to look at the facts that convinced me that we are the chosen generation, the generation that will witness the catching away of the church.

We are going to discuss many things in this book, including some that are not so politically correct:

- Is the rapture a real thing?
- Who is really going to make it to heaven?
- Who is going through the Tribulation?
- What part does Israel play in this process?
- What are the signs of Jesus's appearing?
- Are homosexuality and its derivatives mentioned in the Bible?
- Does the National Security Agency play a part in all of this?

I am so happy that you decided to add this book to your library because I know you will learn a great deal about the time in which you are living. I invite you to open your Bible, get a cup of coffee, take some notes if you want, and increase your awareness of *What's Going On?*

Dr. Ed King

1

ARE WE THE RAPTURE GENERATION?

We are living in a society that is worldwide, not merely a local community. It is our community for sure, but we live in a broader context where world events affect us more quickly than even a few years ago. We are more informed about world events than we have ever been because of mass communications, the internet, and the twenty-four-hour news cycle. As a result, now more than ever, global events tend to have more of a personal impact on us.

We Have a Profound Need for Information

Every day, a tremendous amount of news is generated; some rather ordinary, some quite chaotic. People have always desired information, and that desire has paved the way for the creation of the varied communications technologies that we enjoy on a daily basis. How different our daily lives would be without the internet, smartphones, digital tablets, email, texting, and music technology. Now, we can add computers on our wrists, with products like the Apple Watch, and personal technology, like

Amazon's Echo, which we can command to do everything from telling us the news, time, and weather to turning our lights off at night and locking the front door. I'm even wondering if those famous words, "Beam me up, Scotty," spoken by the crew of the *Starship Enterprise*, will be uttered in our lifetime with the same expectation of results.

Some of the information we seek is relevant and good, while much of it is not. It is not that the news is fundamentally bad; it is that we simply do not know how to interpret it in light of anything eternal. Nevertheless, we still demand it.

That is what we are going to talk about in this book. In the next few chapters, I will offer some context to what is going on in the world today and give you some insight to help you determine the difference between what is truly important and what is not. You will learn what it means to you, to society, and to our eternity.

Are We the Rapture Generation?

The subtitle, *Why I Believe We Are the Rapture Generation,* is taken from scripture. I did not just come up with it as a tantalizing title that would somehow influence you to buy this book. Scripture tells us to provoke one another, as well as others, to godliness and righteousness. That's my purpose.

Without question, I believe that we are that generation. In fact, if you have a decent understanding of world events, it is fairly obvious. It is about the signs. That's what goes on in people's minds—all these signs that we find. Jesus told us that the many signs of the end times would happen before He comes again.

We will hear of wars, rumors of wars, and some false Christs in many places. We find these signs spoken of in many different locations in the Bible, including:

> For there shall arise false Christs, and false prophets, and shall shew great signs and wonders; insomuch that, if it were possible, they shall deceive the very elect. (Matthew 24:24)

> For false Christs and false prophets shall rise, and shall shew signs and wonders, to seduce, if it were possible, even the elect. (Mark 13:22)

> And great earthquakes shall be in divers places, and famines, and pestilences; and fearful sights and great signs shall there be from heaven. (Luke 21:11)

> And there shall be signs in the sun, and in the moon, and in the stars; and upon the earth distress of nations, with perplexity; the sea and the waves roaring. (Luke 21:25)

Let's see how these signs fit together. You may be a member of a group that says, "These signs have been spoken of for hundreds and even thousands of years, so why should we think that today is any different? Why should we believe that we are the rapture generation over any other generation? Why should we consider ourselves a part of that generation, when the Lord could come a thousand years from today?" I understand your questions, but I think an informed look at scripture might cause you to consider a different position.

Be Aware of the Times

Be careful as you read scripture because it is easy to refer to certain events out of context. For example, much of what Jesus taught was to the Jews, clearly because the church age had not yet arrived. Because of that, many of the scriptures that you find concerning the signs of Jesus's second coming are directly communicated to the Jews and not to the church at all. They are not scriptures that would necessarily refer to the catching away of the church.

The Starting Point

We cannot have an informed discussion on the subject of the rapture if we don't know what it is, can we? Notice what the Bible says in 1 Thessalonians 4:16–18:

> For the Lord himself shall descend from heaven with a shout, with the voice of the archangel, and with the trump of God: and the dead in Christ shall rise first:
>
> Then we which are alive and remain shall be caught up together with them in the clouds, to meet the Lord in the air: and so shall we ever be with the Lord.
>
> Wherefore comfort one another with these words.

The Rapture of the Church

The rapture is referred to as the "catching up" or the "snatching away" of the church. 1 Thessalonians is not the only place in the Bible that speaks of the rapture of the church—there are many—but we are looking at this specific reference because it is so succinct, direct, and to the point. Look at 1 Thessalonians 4:17 (emphasis added):

> Then we which are alive and remain **shall be caught up.**

The phrase "caught up" is where the concept of the rapture is found. There are certainly other places in the Bible that reference this as well, but this verse is sufficient for now. Other translations of the Bible reference the "catching away" or being "caught up," like this:

- The Phillips Translation says, "to be swept up."
- Today's English Version says, "to be gathered up."
- The Jerusalem Bible says, "to be taken up."
- The Voice Translation says, "to be snatched up."
- The Knox Translation says, "to be swept away."

You get the concept. The rapture is an unexplainable, instantaneous action that has the power to take us out of the present world as we know it and into an entirely different dimension.

There have been several books written and movies produced over the years that tried to depict what the rapture of the church would look like; some were decent, while others not so much. The successful book and movie series entitled *Left Behind* dealt directly with what it might resemble. It gave us a glimpse of what the world could experience through the process. It looked at the idea of a large group of people who were caught up out of the population as a whole, while the world was still functioning normally, day-to-day.

What Is the Rapture?

The word *rapture* comes from the Latin *raptile* or *rapio*. Both are different forms of the same word, and their use depends on their part of speech. It is important to know whether they are used as a verb, adverb, or noun, as well as their tense—past, present, or future. There are many different forms in which they are used, but in the end, it is the word *rapio* that gives us the English form of the word *rapture* that we are dealing with here. Let's see what the Bible says:

> For the Lord himself shall descend from heaven with a shout, with the voice of the archangel, and with the trump of God: and the dead in Christ shall rise first:
>
> Then we which are alive and remain shall be caught up together with them in the clouds, to meet the Lord in the air: and so shall we ever be with the Lord. (1 Thessalonians 4:16–17)

As we see here, only the dead in Christ will rise—not the dead who have never received Jesus Christ as their Lord. This resurrection is not a general, all-inclusive event where everybody gets to go, but rather a catching-away only for those who are dead in the Lord.

People in heaven still have a body in a sense, just not one in which we are accustomed. At the Resurrection, their heavenly bodies will reunite with their physical remains—left behind at their earthly death—and will unite in the air in a fabulous way.

The Rapture Is Real

You are going to have a real problem with scripture if you don't believe in the rapture of the church. I listened to a very cynical person not too long ago, who declared, "Rapture, rupture; who cares?" What they were trying to say was, "I don't understand all this talk about the end times." The upshot of the whole thing was, "It doesn't even matter."

He was wrong; it does matter. In fact, it matters a great deal. The reason it means so much is because it is the Holy Scriptures we are looking at, and not someone's opinion. So regardless of where you put it in the sequence of time or the order of events as it unfolds throughout our future, you cannot deny the fact that the event called the rapture exists.

There Is a Caveat

When you look at prophetic scripture that references the coming of the Lord, you will not necessarily see the signs related to Christ's appearing as necessarily being signs of the rapture. At Jesus's second coming, every eye will see Him. Let's look at the reference in Revelation, chapter 1:

> Behold, he cometh with clouds; and every eye
> shall see him. (Revelation 1:7)

This verse is referring to the time Jesus comes to set up His kingdom on the earth. That day is coming, but before that happens, the rapture of the church occurs—an entirely different event. When Jesus appears, everyone will see Him like lightning from the east to the west. Look at Matthew 24:27:

> For as the lightning cometh out of the east, and shineth even unto the west; so shall also the coming of the Son of man be.

The previous verse is talking about the coming of the Lord. But before that happens—seven years before that happens—the rapture of the church takes place. That's when the group of people known as the saints of God are caught up with Jesus in the air.

At this point, there will also be a series of occurrences known as the twenty-one judgments—found in Revelation 6–18. As these twenty-one judgments are taking place on the earth, others—the Marriage Supper of the Lamb, in particular—are taking place in heaven.

If Jesus held back the rapture to be a part of His appearing, this Marriage Supper would be considered fast food compared to the glorious event scheduled to take place in heaven. Why? Because after rising to meet the Lord in the air, you would immediately turn around and come back to the earth with Him without stepping one foot into heaven. Theologically, that will not hold water. You would need to eliminate the Marriage Supper of the Lamb to believe that it's all one event. It is not possible to do that using sound doctrine.

Jesus is going to come for the church and then come back with the church; the events are distinctly different. There are many things—both heavenly and earthly—that take place in that span of time, and there are times and seasons for all of them.

Look at 1 Thessalonians 5:1–2 (emphasis added):

> But of the **times and the seasons**, brethren, ye have no need that I write unto you.
>
> For yourselves know perfectly that the day of the Lord so cometh as a thief in the night.

The apostle Paul said that there would be a particular time and season when destruction comes upon the unbelievers but not upon the believers. Some people will escape, while others will not. Notice verse 3:

> For when they shall say, Peace and safety; then sudden destruction cometh upon them, as travail upon a woman with child; and they shall not escape. (1 Thessalonians 5:3)

It is important to notice that sudden destruction comes upon the unbelievers, but it does not touch us. They do not escape. We do.

> Watch ye therefore, and pray always, that ye may be accounted **worthy to escape** all these things that shall come to pass, and to stand before the Son of man. (Luke 21:36, emphasis added)

Just for the Weak?

Some people say that the rapture idea is "just for weak Christians who want to avoid life's problems and take the easy way out. They just want to go away and hide." However, nothing could be further from the truth. It is for smart Christians who know the Bible. I didn't put the word *escape* in that verse. Some people will escape the events that happen in the last days, while others will not.

So who stays and who goes? If we are counted worthy to escape, we will be rescued and delivered from the horrible events that are going to happen. Our prayer should be that we would be counted worthy to escape.

Counted Worthy?

What does scripture mean when it says that we need to be counted worthy? It means being in Christ. Jesus is coming for those of us who are in Him. If you have accepted Jesus Christ as your Lord and Savior, you are born again and counted in the worthy column. You do not have to physically grow up, reach a certain maturity level, or become doctrinally perfect to get there. You just have to be in Christ, and then you're ready. There is nothing to earn here. This is a grace proposition. The Bible says in 1 Thessalonians 5:4:

> But ye, brethren, are not in darkness, that that
> day should overtake you as a thief.

Notice that when that happens, it comes upon the unbelievers as a thief, but not the believers. We are not children of darkness and of night, but children of the light and of the day. He continues:

> Therefore let us not sleep as do others but let us watch and be sober. (1 Thessalonians 5:6)

The Bible tells us that signs are coming. Scripture also says that many disturbing things are going to happen, but as children of light, we'll be able to see the signs and recognize them for what they are. People in the world, who are full of darkness, will not have a clue. The signs will come on them like a thief.

We will see the signs that indicate these activities, but it will not have to take us unaware. We may not know the day or the hour they happen, but we will certainly know the times and the seasons.

2

A GREAT TRIBULATION

Jesus said that there is a Great Tribulation coming upon the earth:

> For then shall be great tribulation, such as was not since the beginning of the world to this time, no, nor ever shall be. (Matthew 24:21)

The Bible tells us the same thing in Revelation 6:17:

> For the great day of his wrath is come; and who shall be able to stand?

The scripture is its own best commentary and defines itself better than anyone else can. The Bible says that for many reasons, the Tribulation period is a time of God's wrath on the earth. In Daniel 9, you can find an excellent explanation of why the Tribulation—the judgment dealing with sin, and all the related consequences—takes place. It tells you why it happens.

"Well, a loving God wouldn't do that," you exclaim. Well, a loving people would not put Him in that position, either. That is not what God wanted to do; it is what we forced Him to do.

For God hath not appointed us to wrath, but to obtain salvation by our Lord Jesus Christ. (1 Thessalonians 5:9)

Who Goes through the Tribulation?

If words mean anything, God's people are in good shape where the Tribulation is concerned. Here's why: As we saw earlier in Revelation 6:17, God said that the Tribulation period was a day of His wrath. Add to that what we just read in 1 Thessalonians—that we have not been appointed to wrath—and the only educated conclusion we can come to is that the church does not go through the Tribulation.

A well-meaning individual once said to me, "I always thought that everyone went through the Tribulation. I've read and studied a lot of this stuff, and that's my honest opinion."

Unfortunately, their thought process was just a bit off. We are discussing what the Bible says about the subject, not our opinion of it. No matter whose opinions they are, they are subject to the Bible, not the other way around. They do not matter even a little unless they are established and proven by the Word of God.

We Need Absolutes

We should never wrestle with scripture just to get it to say what we want. If we try to allegorize the scripture—shaping it into something more palatable to us—then we have lost the benefit of seeing it as the authority in our lives.

"So Dr. King," you say, "because of what you said, I assume you believe in a literal interpretation of the Bible."

Do I have another choice? There is no other choice for a Christian. I am not going to make this stuff up.

I can just hear the conversation:

"Well, what does that mean to you?"

"You tell me first; what does it mean to you?"

"I asked you before you asked me; what does it mean to you?"

I am going to tell you what it means to all of us when you take that view; it means nothing. The Bible says the scripture is of no private interpretation.

However, there is specialized attention that the Holy Spirit can give to a message to personalize it to each of us. Scripture becomes personal and private in how I deal with it, but the scripture is no one's opinion. God meant what He said, and He did not mean something else. If God did not mean what He said, then why didn't He say what He meant? Knowing that God is neither stupid nor confused, I know that He meant every word of it.

Through study, analysis, and help from the Holy Spirit, we have the opportunity to look at these things and figure out precisely what God meant. However, because these subjects are tedious, they take a great deal of work to finish, and some people tend to be lazy. Their plans for following through on a thorough study of scripture tend to stall long before it's complete.

A Time of God's Wrath

The Tribulation period is a time of God's wrath on the earth. It is a seven-year stretch broken down into two three-and-a-half-year segments, calculated in Jewish years (which consist of 360 days each). It is not only a period of God's wrath; it's also the time of the antichrist, who will be revealed at God's discretion.

The antichrist appears at the beginning of that seven-year period on a platform of peace. After three and a half years, he sits in the Temple and declares himself to be God. He becomes the "abomination that maketh desolate," or what we refer to as the Abomination of Desolation. He will break his covenant of peace with the Jewish people, which results in extreme upheaval on the earth. (Note: Some scholars refer to the Tribulation as the full seven-year period, while others refer to it as the last half of that seven-year period.) The Bible refers to it as the time of Jacob's trouble. Look at Jeremiah 30:7:

> Alas! for that day is great, so that none is like it: it is even the time of Jacob's trouble, but he shall be saved out of it.

In Genesis 32:28, God changed Jacob's name:

> And he said, Thy name shall be called no more Jacob, but Israel: for as a prince hast thou power with God and with men, and hast prevailed.

Jacob Becomes Israel

God changed Jacob's name to Israel, and as a result, the names Jacob and Israel became synonymous. So if it's a time of Jacob's trouble, it's a time of Israel's trouble. It's not a time that God judges His church, but a season of God dealing with the Jews. The Jews brought this upon themselves because they, unlike the church, rejected Jesus's first coming. You had to accept His first coming to be a part of the church. If you rejected it like the Jews, you are not born again. On the other hand, people who did accept His first coming became born again and subsequently became a part of the church.

Without establishing a foundation from which to work, it would be impossible to make a case for why I believe we are the rapture generation. You cannot have an intelligent discussion concerning it or the Tribulation if nobody knows what they are. A solid base needs to be established.

This is the fundamental lesson that sets the foundation. It's very similar to building a house. The most important aspect of constructing a house is first creating a strong, rock-hard, and well-constructed foundation. The remainder of this book will be built from it. I am going to give you some very distinct and definite signs as we go along.

In Matthew 24:32–35, Jesus was teaching about the fig tree:

> Now learn a parable of the fig tree; When his branch is yet tender, and putteth forth leaves, ye know that summer is nigh:

> So likewise ye, when ye shall see all these things, know that it is near, even at the doors.
>
> Verily I say unto you, This generation shall not pass, till all these things be fulfilled.
>
> Heaven and earth shall pass away, but my words shall not pass away.

I can validate the provocative statement, "I believe that we are the rapture generation," by those verses right there. Verse 34 is vitally important and telling:

> This generation shall not pass, till all these things be fulfilled. (Matthew 24:34)

If you are correctly interpreting what you see, and you are there to watch it begin, not a generation will pass until you see it all. If you accurately understand the signs in front of you, it is not presumptuous to believe that you are the generation we are talking about. In fact, even though many overconfident critics—who think they know infinitely more than they actually do—have much to say to the contrary, it would be irresponsible not to say it. There are definite signs, and anybody who is the least bit spiritually discerning can recognize them if they know what to look for.

The Law of First Mention

As we just read, one of the signs that Jesus spoke of was the fig tree. Speaking of the tree, there is a concept in the Bible called the Law of First Mention. For example, in Genesis 1:28, God blessed Adam:

> And God blessed them, and God said unto them, Be fruitful, and multiply, and replenish the earth, and subdue it:

Unless God restates the blessing every time He speaks it to man, what He said in the 28th verse of Genesis is exactly what He meant. That's the blessing He spoke over man initially, and every time He blessed him after that, He meant the same thing: "Be fruitful, and multiply, and replenish the earth, and subdue it."

When you bless someone, you need to mean what you say too. When you say, "Bless you," to someone, it should mean more than a cliché directed at someone who just sneezed.

3

God Gives Us Signs

What Is a Sign?

Before we get too far into the chapter, it might be good to know what the word *sign* really means.

The word *sign* is defined as

- a mark,
- an indicator,
- something that signifies something,
- a means to distinguish or to authenticate something,
- a token, or
- an indication of a coming event or an announcement.

The Parable of the Fig Tree

Jesus said to learn the parable of the fig tree because it is one of the signs. Remembering the Law of First Mention and the Bible being its own best commentary, what Jesus said initially will be what carries on through. There is no restatement necessary.

Sometimes, the fig tree is a type, but other times it may be an actual fig tree; if you remember, Jesus once spoke to a fig tree and cursed it. That tree was once abounding with fruit, but because of Jesus's words, it died from the roots up and never again produced fruit.

Before He spoke to the fig tree, Jesus had been at the Temple, where He overturned the moneychanger's tables. So He was also cursing in typology, the failing religious system adopted by the Jewish people that resulted in the traditions of men making the Word of God of none effect. He was cursing a system as well as a real fig tree. In that case, it had dual meanings. The point here is that Jesus was associating Israel with the fig tree.

Let's look at Hosea 9:10, where God said,

> I found Israel like grapes in the wilderness; I saw your fathers as the firstripe in the fig tree at her first time.

The takeaway here should be that God found Israel like grapes in the wilderness—like the first ripe fruit of the fig tree. He was saying that Israel was and is the fig tree.

A Nation Came upon His Land

> **For a nation is come up upon my land**, strong, and without number, whose teeth are the teeth of a lion, and he hath the cheek teeth of a great lion. (Joel 1:6, emphasis added)

God said that a nation had invaded His covenant land, the land that He gave to Abram. (It wasn't until Genesis 17:5 that God changed Abram's name to Abraham, the father of many nations). God had told him to go out and look around, and whatever he saw, He was going to give it to him. God was going to bless the land. There would be some boundaries involved, but the real estate would be his. Here is what God said to Abram when He gave him all that property:

> And the Lord said unto Abram, after that Lot was separated from him, Lift up now thine eyes, and look from the place where thou art northward, and southward, and eastward, and westward:
>
> For all the land which thou seest, to thee will I give it, and to thy seed for ever.
>
> And I will make thy seed as the dust of the earth: so that if a man can number the dust of the earth, then shall thy seed also be numbered.
>
> Arise, walk through the land in the length of it and in the breadth of it; for I will give it unto thee. (Genesis 13:14–17)

Let's go on to verse 7 in the book of Joel we referenced above:

> He hath laid my vine waste, and barked my fig tree. (Joel 1:7a)

God said that the nation that came against His land also came against His fig tree. Because of that statement, we can positively conclude that the land of Israel—the nation of Israel—is God's fig tree; no question about it. As Jesus said,

> Now learn a parable of the fig tree; When his branch is yet tender, and putteth forth leaves, ye know that summer is nigh. (Matthew 24:32)

That was the first instance of what we can look back on that says to us that we are the rapture generation. In the next verse, He said:

> So likewise ye, when ye shall see all these things, know that it is near, even at the doors. (Matthew 24:33)

When the signs that God gives us begin, not a generation will pass until it is all done. When it starts, it is not going to stop until it is all fulfilled.

The fulfillment, as far as we are concerned, is the appearing of the Lord. However, at the time between the beginning of all these signs and the appearance of Jesus—when every eye shall see and behold Him—the rapture of the church takes place. The closer we get to witness the signs of His appearing, get ready, because before that happens, the church is raptured.

Not a generation will pass until it is all fulfilled. Jesus said in Matthew 16:2–3,

> He answered and said unto them, When it is evening, ye say, It will be fair weather: for the sky is red.

And in the morning, It will be foul weather
to day: for the sky is red and lowering (or
threatening). O ye hypocrites, ye can discern
the face of the sky; but can ye not discern the
signs of the times?

Jesus said that you are a hypocrite if you can't figure it out.
Not my words. Jesus also said it is hypocritical to act like you
don't know what you really do know. We spend more time
trying to understand earthly signs like the weather, than on the
more significant signs of the end times. The weather seems to
attract our attention to a higher degree than important spiritual
matters. We should know this. Jesus calls it hypocritical not to.

Did you listen to the weather report this morning? I look at
the weather report first thing every day—after prayer and Bible
study, of course. It's important to me because I want to know
what the weather is going to be like when I walk out of the
house. Will I need a heavy coat, or would shorts and a golf shirt
be more appropriate?

We watch the weather because it affects our lives. God says
that if you keep track of the weather, you should also keep an
eye on the signs of the times. That is the lesson here. There is
nothing that God does not want us to know if we are responsible
thinkers. He not only wants us to know these things, but He
also desires to help us find them by giving us a roadmap. Notice
what He said in the last part of Matthew 16:3:

O ye hypocrites, ye can discern the face of the
sky; but can ye not discern the signs of the
times?

It takes some discernment to understand the times in which we live. In this book, I am helping you enhance your spiritual understanding and insight, so you'll be able to comprehend more effectively what's going on in your world. This information will help you recognize the signs of the times in which you live.

In Acts 2, the Bible says that God is going to show us some incredible signs and wonders in the last days:

> And it shall come to pass in the last days, saith God …
>
> And I will shew wonders in heaven above, and signs in the earth beneath. (Acts 2:17a, 19a)

A friend called me some time back and told me that he had just discovered the Blood Moon phenomenon. He said, "Do you believe that God could give us a sign like that? Do you believe this could be happening?" He wasn't joking around, either. He was digging into it.

I replied, "I do believe it. Absolutely. I don't precisely know what it all means, but I don't doubt for a second that the Lord is talking to us. In fact, I think God is talking to all of humankind all the time; I just don't think we're listening."

God is talking loud and clear, but we, as a people, seem to be deaf as a hammer. In Acts, chapter 2, God told us that He would show us wonders in the heavens above and signs in the earth beneath. So there are many ways that He wants to show us signs.

God is announcing what He is doing, but it takes a discerning ear to hear it. He is declaring that Jesus is coming, so we need to be ready to receive Him. However, Jesus is coming at His appointed time, whether we are prepared for Him or not. He is not going to wait for us to get our lives in order. He is on His way. Be assured that He is returning.

4

REASONS WHY WE ARE "THE" GENERATION

It All Starts with Israel

The first reason why I believe that we are the rapture generation—according to what Jesus said, not according to what I think—happened on May 15, 1948, when Israel was restored as a nation. That one event is the foundational sign that brings all the other signs to an elevated level of importance.

Throughout ancient history, there have been reports of devastating earthquakes, volcanoes, and all types of natural disasters. Volcanoes and earthquakes go hand-in-hand in scripture to the point of interchangeability. There have also been events that Jesus spoke of, like wars, rumors of wars, signs in the Heavenlies, and many other occurrences, however relevant and important to us, that were all lacking in end-times prophetic significance until Israel once again became a nation. It was impossible for the generation that Jesus was referring to, to be the rapture generation until Israel was reunited and restored. As a result, those events were less significant then than they are today.

God Scatters and Gathers

The children of Israel were a very disobedient people to the Lord on many occasions. Sounds a little bit like America, doesn't it (over 75 million or so aborted babies and many other things)? We don't have a finger to point at anybody. Because of their disobedience, the Lord said some things about them and to them. Let's look at what was said in Deuteronomy 28:64 (emphasis added):

> And **the Lord shall scatter thee** among all people, from the one end of the earth even unto the other; and there thou shalt serve other gods, which neither thou nor thy fathers have known, even wood and stone.

The point I want to make here is that God prophesied that He would scatter the Jewish people. They were taken captive into Babylon and stayed there for seventy years until they were restored as a nation. Look at the next verse:

> And among these nations shalt thou find no ease, neither shall the sole of thy foot have rest: but the Lord shall give thee there a trembling heart, and failing of eyes, and sorrow of mind. (Deuteronomy 28:65)

This judgment was real. Because of the Jews' sin and disobedience to God, they were scattered among all the people of the earth. This scattering was global. In verse 66, the judgment became even more serious (if that were possible):

And thy life shall hang in doubt before thee; and thou shalt fear day and night, and shalt have none assurance of thy life. (Deuteronomy 28:66, emphasis added)

The Jews were scattered to the four winds as judgment for their sins, but as prophesied, God, in His mercy, gathered them together again from every nation of the earth. Let's look at Deuteronomy 30:3, 5:

That then the Lord thy God will turn thy captivity, and have compassion upon thee, and will return and gather thee from all the nations, whither the Lord thy God hath scattered thee.…

And the Lord thy God will bring thee into the land which thy fathers possessed, and thou shalt possess it; and he will do thee good, and multiply thee above thy fathers.

These verses in Deuteronomy mention both the scattering and the gathering of the Jews. Realize, however, that when they were scattered, the earthquakes, wars, and famines that Jesus talked about could not possibly have been part of the rapture generation because the Jews had not been gathered together again; they had not been restored as a nation.

Remember what Jesus said in Matthew 24:32–34:

Now learn a parable of the fig tree; When his branch is yet tender, and putteth forth leaves, ye know that summer is nigh:

> So likewise ye, when ye shall see all these things,
> know that it is near, even at the doors.
>
> Verily I say unto you, This generation shall not
> pass, till all these things be fulfilled.

Jesus said to watch the fig tree, because when you see it bud—when you notice the nation of Israel gathered together again—you will begin to see something different happening. After the children of Israel were brought back together from all nations, things began to be different. Things got serious. In fact, this was prophesied back in the Old Testament, in the book of Isaiah:

> And he shall set up an ensign for the nations
> and shall assemble the outcasts of Israel, and
> gather together the dispersed of Judah from the
> four corners of the earth. (Isaiah 11:12)

God said that He would unite His children from the four corners of the earth—not just from Babylon, but from the entire globe. God is gathering the nation of Israel. Jeremiah 23:3 says this:

> And I will gather the remnant of my flock out
> of all countries whither I have driven them and
> will bring them again to their folds, and they
> shall be fruitful and increase.

If you look at Ezekiel 37, God told Ezekiel to prophesy over a valley of old, dry bones, which was the nation of Israel. God said that He would gather them together and bring them back as a nation—the nation of Israel.

Replacement Theology

The amount of theological nonsense there is in the world today is astonishing. It causes extensive misunderstanding of prophetic scripture. One culprit has the name "Replacement Theology," which says the nation of Israel and the word *church* should be used interchangeably. Every time you see the word *church*, you should substitute the word *Israel* in its place, and vice versa. The problem is that it leaves us hopelessly in the dark. I believe without question that this type of prophetic interpretation is a satanic scheme to keep the people of God in total darkness about what is going on.

The Chosen Nation

You are kidding yourself if you do not think Israel is a chosen nation, a chosen generation.

"Wait just a minute," you say. "The church—us, you and me—we're the blessed ones; we're the elect of God."

That is true, but in fact, God has two elects in the Bible. He told Abram to "go out and look up." He said, "I'm going to make your seed as the stars." Then God said, "I want you to look down here at the seashore." He then went further and said, "I want you to pay particular attention at the sand of the seashore; I'm going to make your seed as the grains of sand."

When God said that, He was saying that you have both a spiritual seed and an earthly seed—a spiritual elect and an earthly elect. The church is not the land of Israel, nor is the land of Israel the church. They are not the same, and you need to know which elect God is referring to when He says "the elect." And the only way you can tell which elect He is talking about is in the context. To say point-blank that every time He talks about the elect of God He is talking about the church is wrong. Again, it depends on the context; you must be diligent in your Bible study to know the difference.

Let the Scattering Begin

In 63 BC, a Roman general and statesman, Pompeius, went to Jerusalem and took away the Jews. Known as Pompey the Great, he conquered Jerusalem in a military action known as the Siege of Jerusalem. For 2,011 years, the children of Israel were scattered, controlled not only by Pompey but by other empires of the world as well.

Then things began to change. Let's take a look at the redemptive process of the children of Israel:

> Come, and let us return unto the Lord: for he hath torn, and he will heal us; he hath smitten, and he will bind us up.

> After two days will he revive us: in the third day he will raise us up, and we shall live in his sight. (Hosea 6:1–2)

Psalm 90:4 and 2 Peter 3:8, are similar but just a bit different:

> For a thousand years in thy sight are but as yesterday when it is past, and as a watch in the night. (Psalm 90:4)

But, beloved, be not ignorant of this one thing:

One day is with the Lord as a thousand years,
and a thousand years as one day. (2 Peter 3:8)

Let the Gathering Begin

In 63 BC, the process of scattering the Jews into captivity began. Then, 2,011 years later—or two days, according to Hosea 6—on May 14, 1948, the gathering process began. The children of Israel were revived as a people and came back as a nation. That is the part A of the rapture generation: the restoration of the Jewish people to their homeland, and the part that started the countdown to restoration.

Part B is found here:

And they shall fall by the edge of the sword, and shall be led away captive into all nations: and Jerusalem shall be trodden down of the Gentiles, until the times of the Gentiles be fulfilled. (Luke 21:24)

The phrase "the times of the Gentiles" refers to what we call the church age or the grace age. It is the time of the Gentiles. God dealt with the Jews by blinding them to the changes that were taking place—namely, the many Gentiles who were receiving salvation. This period started about two thousand years ago, and taking into consideration some calendar errors, I believe we are right on the cusp of the rapture. Right on the edge. The church age is getting ready to end, and the time that scripture calls Jacob's trouble is about to begin. It is a time when God deals with the Jews and ceases to deal with the church. It will be called the times of the Gentiles when it is fulfilled, but we will miss it because we will be in heaven.

The gears are meshing and turning, but there is some overlap. It's not one thing one day, and another thing immediately happens the next day. It is much like the changing of seasons—winter fades out over time, and spring gradually fades in. We experience some warm days as winter wraps up and some very cold days even after spring begins. The calendar is precise, but the actual event has some holes and discrepancies in it. Punxsutawney Phil, the famous groundhog, can't tell us for sure when winter is over. He tries but doesn't get it right all the time; his shadow sometimes fails him. In the same way, an overlap of events stops one age and starts another.

The times of the Gentiles began to end when Jerusalem was returned to Israel. Their restoration was in two parts: The first part happened when they got their land back. The second piece occurred in 1967, when they got Jerusalem back. It's important to remember that the generational countdown started in 1967, not 1948.

It's in the Generations

Edgar Whisenant, the man who wrote *88 Reasons Why the Rapture Could be in 1988*, based his numbers on his belief that a generation equaled forty years. He based that on the forty years that the children of Israel wandered in the wilderness. He took that forty-year number, overlaid it on the year 1948, and came up with 1988. Sounds plausible, but it is not accurate.

There are problems with that particular interpretation of the numbers—the first being that the countdown should not have started until 1967, and second, there is no way of knowing precisely the number of years in a generation. Could it then be 120 years, based on the book of Genesis and the days of a man being 120 years? Could it be? I don't think so.

And the Answer Is …

If you look at the number of people and the number of years that transpired throughout the genealogies of Jesus, you will come up with a division. It is nothing more than a math problem. You will discover a generational number of about fifty-two to fifty-three years. Plugging in that figure starting in 1967—the year that Israel got her land back—it would work out like this: 1967 plus fifty-two years would work out to be the year 2019. Using the fifty-three-year generational number, the year 2020 would be the target. Check the math if you must, but I'm right. We are on the cusp.

God said that not a generation would pass until it all happens. We are the generation, regardless of how we calculate it. Jesus is coming very soon, and it could be tonight. I don't know if I'm correct down to the day and the hour, but I'm close.

We are the rapture generation.

5

DIVIDING THE LAND

Where Our Covenant Began

Although our covenant has gone through different stages down through history, we are told in the New Testament to follow the faith of Abraham—the father of our faith—as our current covenant began with him. Abraham's faith was transferred into his descendants, into the Jewish people, and finally into the church. It was not just for them; it was for us, as well.

Look at Genesis 12:1–2:

> Now the Lord had said unto Abram, Get thee out of thy country, and from thy kindred, and from thy father's house, unto a land that I will shew thee:
>
> And I will make of thee a great nation, and I will bless thee, and make thy name great; and thou shalt be a blessing.

God told Abram to leave his home country and his people behind and move to a land of the Lord's choosing. If Abram followed God's directions, he would become the father of a great nation; he would be blessed and famous, and become a blessing to many other people. God said this:

> And I will bless them that bless thee, and curse him that curseth thee: and in thee shall all families of the earth be blessed. (Genesis 12:3)

God went on to say that He would bless anyone who blessed Abram and curse anyone who cursed him. God also said that, because of him, the entire world would be blessed.

Two Types of Seed

When all of this took place, the nation of Israel did not exist, nor was there a Jewish people. The land and the people came directly out of this covenant. Look at Genesis 12:7:

> And the Lord appeared unto Abram, and said, Unto thy seed will I give this land: and there builded he an altar unto the Lord, who appeared unto him.

The first part of verse 7 has created quite a bit of controversy. God said that He would give the land to Abram's descendants. However, even in the church world, there is a good deal of internal conflict about whether the Jewish people—the children of Israel—are actually God's chosen people. Through nothing more than a casual attempt at Bible study, I can certainly understand how the conclusion could be reached that the church has replaced the Jewish people as God's chosen. I also realize how some of the disagreement over this issue has happened—that the elect of the old covenant is not the elect of the new covenant. I get that. I don't agree with it, but I get it.

Abram's seed is represented by the earthly seed—represented by the number of the grains of sand of the seashore—and the spiritual seed—expressed as the number of stars in the heavens. God told Abram that his offspring would be representative of both.

God Makes a Promise

In Genesis 13:14–17, God makes a promise to Abram about the land:

> And the Lord said unto Abram, after that Lot was separated from him, Lift up now thine eyes, and look from the place where thou art northward, and southward, and eastward, and westward:
>
> For all the land which thou seest, to thee will I give it, and to thy seed for ever.
>
> And I will make thy seed as the dust of the earth: so that if a man can number the dust of the earth, then shall thy seed also be numbered.
>
> Arise, walk through the land in the length of it and in the breadth of it; for I will give it unto thee.

Verse 15 says that God would give all the land that Abram could see to his offspring forever. It would be both his and his heirs—his heritage and his legacy to his descendants. Don't disregard the word *forever*. Think about that. Forever. A long, long, time that never ends.

Some say that God changed His decision at the cross because the Jews rejected Jesus, but try as you might, you cannot find any record of it. It's just not there. Also, there are those who claim that keeping the land was conditional—and they would be right. The Jews were exiled from their land for not following the rules, so to speak, but they eventually came back because God restored them. Look at what God says in Genesis 17:7–8:

> And I will establish my covenant between me and thee and thy seed after thee in their generations for an everlasting covenant, to be a God unto thee, and to thy seed after thee.

> And I will give unto thee, and to thy seed after thee, the land wherein thou art a stranger, all the land of Canaan, for an everlasting possession; and I will be their God.

That is as clear as it gets. God said, "I will give the land to you and your seed for an everlasting possession." God Almighty said that—not the United States government, the United Nations, Great Britain, or the European Union. Consequently, since they did not say it, they do not have the power to change anything.

When you dishonor God and His Word, you don't care about things like that, because you don't believe it matters. But know this: God defends His Word and watches over it to make sure that He performs what it contains. I don't care how self-confident you think you are, hitting God cross-grain will put you on the losing side every time.

You may honestly believe that either the God of the Bible is dead or He is nothing more than a figment of someone's imagination. He is nothing more in your eyes than a big fairy tale. Well, you are getting ready to find out what these so-called fairy tales really are. They are not anything close to what you think. The fairy tale, in this case, is your belief that you are bigger and better than God is. The fairy tale is to believe that anybody, any organization, or any group of people can outsmart, outthink, or outmaneuver Him. God sits in the Heavenlies and laughs at those who think they can outdo Him.

God Will Remember His Covenant

Look at this passage from Leviticus 26:42:

> Then will I remember my covenant with Jacob, and also my covenant with Isaac, and also my covenant with Abraham will I remember; and I will remember the land.

God said that this covenant was everlasting and eternal with the people and with the land. Notice, however, that this passage tells of a covenant not only with Abraham but with Isaac and Jacob, as well.

Ishmael was another of Abraham's sons. Ishmael was born to Hagar, which resulted in a conflict—in the minds of some—of rightful heirs. This dispute is significant because some people say that Ishmael is the son who was the legitimate heir of the covenant, but they are wrong. Although God informed Ishmael that He was going to bless him with an abundance of descendants, God's covenant promise was going to come through Isaac. Through Isaac, it was passed on to Jacob, who God renamed Israel. The covenant line was now Abraham, Isaac, and Israel. It is essential that you recognize this lineage because there are numerous conflicts concerning it. Let's look at the account in Psalm 105:8–12:

> He hath remembered his covenant for ever, the word which he commanded to a thousand generations.
>
> Which covenant he made with Abraham, and his oath unto Isaac;
>
> And confirmed the same unto Jacob for a law, and to Israel for an everlasting covenant:
>
> Saying, Unto thee will I give the land of Canaan, the lot of your inheritance:
>
> When they were but a few men in number; yea, very few, and strangers in it.

God said that He was giving Abraham the land that we refer to as the land of Canaan—the Promised Land. He made that covenant with them when they were just a few men. God initially started with Abraham when He said, "Abraham, I'm going to give you the land." Then it passed on to his seed, Isaac, and then to his seed, Jacob, who later became Israel.

We hear about it all through scripture. That promise hasn't been rendered null and void; it is still alive and well. God is not through with this thing yet, as this is an everlasting promise and an everlasting covenant with the land. Look at verse 11 again:

> Saying, Unto thee will I give the land of Canaan, the lot of your inheritance. (Psalm 105:11)

In other words, God was saying that He would give Abraham the land of Israel for his inheritance. Let's look at Ezekiel 36:24, where God promises to bring Abraham into his land:

> For I will take you from among the heathen, and gather you out of all countries, and will bring you into your own land.

6

THE VALLEY OF DRY BONES

In the book of Ezekiel, we are beginning to see an unfolding story starting in chapters 36 and 37 of the prophet Ezekiel's vision of the Valley of Dry Bones. Here is his account:

> The hand of the Lord was upon me, and carried me out in the spirit of the Lord, and set me down in the midst of the valley which was full of bones,
>
> And caused me to pass by them round about: and, behold, there were very many in the open valley; and, lo, they were very dry.
>
> And he said unto me, Son of man, can these bones live? And I answered, O Lord God, thou knowest.
>
> Again he said unto me, Prophesy upon these bones, and say unto them, O ye dry bones, hear the word of the Lord.

Thus saith the Lord God unto these bones; Behold, I will cause breath to enter into you, and ye shall live:

And I will lay sinews upon you, and will bring up flesh upon you, and cover you with skin, and put breath in you, and ye shall live; and ye shall know that I am the Lord.

So I prophesied as I was commanded: and as I prophesied, there was a noise, and behold a shaking, and the bones came together, bone to his bone.

And when I beheld, lo, the sinews and the flesh came up upon them, and the skin covered them above: but there was no breath in them.

Then said he unto me, Prophesy unto the wind, prophesy, son of man, and say to the wind, Thus saith the Lord God; Come from the four winds, O breath, and breathe upon these slain, that they may live.

So I prophesied as he commanded me, and the breath came into them, and they lived, and stood up upon their feet, an exceeding great army.

Then he said unto me, Son of man, these bones are the whole house of Israel: behold, they say, Our bones are dried, and our hope is lost: we are cut off for our parts.

> Therefore prophesy and say unto them, Thus saith the Lord God; Behold, O my people, I will open your graves, and cause you to come up out of your graves, and bring you into the land of Israel.

> And ye shall know that I am the Lord, when I have opened your graves, O my people, and brought you up out of your graves,

> And shall put my spirit in you, and ye shall live, and I shall place you in your own land: then shall ye know that I the Lord have spoken it, and performed it, saith the Lord. (Ezekiel 37:1–14)

In the vision, God was telling all His people that He was going to round them up from the many nations where they had been scattered over the last two thousand years. He said that He was going to bring them back into the land that was promised to them—bone to bone, bone to bone.

Here is what Ezekiel prophesied in the vision:

> So I prophesied as I was commanded: and as I prophesied, there was a noise, and behold a shaking, and the bones came together, bone to his bone.

> And when I beheld, lo, the sinews and the flesh came up upon them, and the skin covered them above: but there was no breath in them.

Then said he unto me, Prophesy unto the wind, prophesy, son of man, and say to the wind, Thus saith the Lord God; Come from the four winds, O breath, and breathe upon these slain, that they may live.

So I prophesied as he commanded me, and the breath came into them, and they lived, and stood up upon their feet, an exceeding great army. (Ezekiel 37:7–10)

The bones came together and began to form a skeletal structure. Muscle and flesh formed over the bones, and skin covered them. Finally, God commanded Ezekiel to prophesy to the wind to breathe on the dead so life would come into the bodies. The dead came alive, stood on their feet, and became a great army. It is representative, according to scripture, of the nation of Israel. In Ezekiel 36:28:

And you shall dwell in the land that I gave to your fathers; and you shall be my people, and I will be your God.

They will dwell in their land.

Then he said unto me, Son of man, these bones are the whole house of Israel. (Ezekiel 37:11)

God said that the bones represented the nation of Israel— the reassembling of the people into their land. This is more than just an opinion from some random theologian trying to interpret its meaning.

From Israel to His Coming

All prophetic scripture in Matthew 24, Luke 21, and other places contain what Jesus said referring to the events leading up to the appearing of the Lord. We see these things funneling us in and taking us to that day, which started when the Jewish people were reinstated to the land that God promised them.

> Thus saith the Lord God; Behold, I will take the children of Israel from among the heathen, whither they be gone, and will gather them on every side, and bring them into their own land. (Ezekiel 37:21)

Are you getting the drift? Are you beginning to see a pattern emerge? The conversation is about their land. Not our land, but their land: the land of Israel.

Israel is prophetic land. The United States, Great Britain, and Hong Kong are not prophetically significant areas in this conversation. These countries may have something do with the unfolding of scripture over time, but they are not included in the land promised by God to the Jewish people. Israel is the only nation that is considered God's covenant land. Israel is God's choice; according to scripture, it's the navel of the earth. It is a strategic location for a vital time, and God will not allow it to be overrun or taken from His children, period. He will not permit His covenant—which this land is a strategic part of—to become invalidated. Doing anything designed to remove Israel from their land is to come against the God of the Bible.

The Two-State Solution

During the Obama administration, the United Nations was trying very hard to muscle through legislation that would allow the Palestinians to possess a portion of Jewish land. They were not trying to push the Jews entirely off the land; they just wanted to give a significant piece of it to the Palestinian people. It would mean that the Jews had to share the area—which God promised only to them—with the Palestinians.

A part of the two-state solution that was being discussed was dividing the city of Jerusalem—even though many Christians, Jews, Arabs, and Muslims currently live there together, side-by-side, peacefully, with no conflict at all. However, it does make for a long religious weekend: the Muslims get Friday, the Jews get Saturday, and the Christians get Sunday.

Israel is being pressed on all sides to give up portions of their land. The United Nations and the European Union are pushing it. Even France made a particularly strong attempt to get Israel to give back pre-1967 boundaries, which included the West Bank. Add to that the ongoing conflict concerning the Gaza Strip.

The United States has been pushing this particular peace process as well, with most of the negotiations requiring land for peace. They say that Israel must give up some amount of its God-ordained land to deflect further conflict. That idea is highly improbable, however, when the people and nations around them don't want anything to do with peace. When the people at the table are determined to destroy you, it is pretty much impossible to negotiate peace. This next verse sums it up quite nicely:

> They have said, Come, let us cut them off from
> being a nation; that the name of Israel may be
> no more in remembrance. (Psalm 83:4)

It's Getting Clearer

Here is what some national news outlets had to say concerning the issue of a two-state solution:

One newscaster said that Israeli's prime minister, Benjamin Netanyahu (in statements made the day before, and then shortly after his reelection in 2009), remarked that he didn't see a Palestinian state happening. Another said that the White House commented that the United States might now stop protecting Israel—a reversal of decades of US policy.

Still another commented that in spite of Netanyahu's overwhelming victory, President Obama refused to pick up the phone to congratulate him. However, Obama later took the time to address the people of Iran—one of America's worst enemies—but did not even speak to the leadership of Israel, one of America's closest allies.

So the question remains, "What's going on?" I hope the answer is becoming clearer. When you speak directly from scripture, it helps put into context what you are seeing. Much of the country—the dope-smoking, oblivious to reality, video game playing, lost in social media element—cannot see their hands in front of their faces.

That is the purpose of this book. People need to know what is going on in the world today. Some people in the United States, as well as other countries around the world, are pushing for this ungodly takeover. We are neck deep in it. This is not a game. It is your country as much as it is others.

Isaiah 41:8–9 is even more revealing:

> But thou, Israel, art my servant, Jacob whom I have chosen, the seed of Abraham my friend.
>
> Thou whom I have taken from the ends of the earth, and called thee from the chief men thereof, and said unto thee,
>
> Thou art my servant; I have chosen thee, and not cast thee away.

That tells you very clearly that God has not cast Israel away. Verse 9 flies in the face of Replacement Theology, which would say to you that, in fact, He has. Unlike some theologians would have you believe, God has not discarded Israel. Look at the next verses:

> Fear thou not; for I am with thee: be not dismayed; for I am thy God: I will strengthen thee; yea, I will help thee; yea, I will uphold thee with the right hand of my righteousness.
>
> Behold, all they that were incensed against thee shall be ashamed and confounded: they shall be as nothing; and they that strive with thee shall perish. (Isaiah 41:10–11)

I do not care how powerful and mighty you think you are; you are nowhere close to that. Let's go on to the next couple of verses:

> Thou shalt seek them, and shalt not find them, even them that contended with thee: they that war against thee shall be as nothing, and as a thing of nought.

> For I the Lord thy God will hold thy right hand, saying unto thee, Fear not; I will help thee. (Isaiah 41:12–13)

That is exactly what people will face when they come against the covenant that God made with His people. Because of my respect for the God of the Bible, I would be afraid to do it. I would never do that. Don't take this the wrong way, but I'm just too smart to do it.

It should be noted that our current president, Donald J. Trump, is a much better friend to Israel than former president Barak Obama ever was. President Trump put meat on the bones of the relationship between the two countries in 2018, by moving the US Embassy from Tel Aviv to Jerusalem, Israel's capital.

7

THERE ARE NO COINCIDENCES

America Needs to Choose Wisely

Let me share some headlines with you that I'm sure you'll find interesting.

May 19, 2011, CNSNews.com

> "Obama Wants Israel to Cede the Palestinian Demand for 1967 Borders."

At that time, President Obama was putting pressure on the Israelis to go back to their 1967 borders, even though Prime Minister Netanyahu has said on more than one occasion that a withdrawal to these borders would keep Israel from effectively defending itself.

This process was being manipulated through money, through the military, and through trade, among other things. There was an aggressive diplomatic push at work. Here are two more:

March 7, 2013, *FrontPage Magazine*

"Obama to Demand Israel Withdraw from Judea and Samaria."

March 23, 2015, BeforeItsNews.com

"Obama Now Demands Israel Give Up Their Land to Create a Palestinian State."

Pressure, and more pressure.

Putting pressure on Israel to divide their land will come with some consequences. There are two books that I would highly recommend that you read on this subject. The first is *God's Final Warning to America*, by John McTernan, and the second is *Eye to Eye* by William R. Koenig. In his book and on his website, Koenig documents many of these types of events—there are around ninety of them—and I want to point out a few of these to you. However, before I do, let's look in the first chapter of the book of Obadiah:

> For the day of the Lord is near upon all the heathen: as thou hast done, it shall be done unto thee: thy reward shall return upon thine own head. (Obadiah 1:15)

You don't have to be a world-renowned theologian to figure this out. Whatever you do to them, the same will be done to you—maybe worse. If you mistreat Israel, your life is going to change for the worse. Going against Israel is something I would never do.

Cause and Effect

Here are a few of the many events mentioned in Koenig's book; you probably remember some of them. We are going to associate the events with the disastrous outcomes that came as a result. I believe you will make the connection, as I did, that decisions that are detrimental to Israel—God's chosen people—can have devastating consequences.

Event #1

> October 30, 1991: President George H.W. Bush—father of President George W. Bush—opened the Madrid Conference with his "Land for Peace" initiative, a Middle East peace plan that required Israel to give up its land.
>
> On the same day, an extremely rare storm formed off the coast of Nova Scotia and produced record-setting hundred-foot waves. It pounded the New England coast, causing heavy damage to President Bush's home in Kennebunkport, Maine. That violent weather front became known as "the Perfect Storm" and was so significant that a hugely successful book and movie originated from it. Coincidence?

Event #2

August 23, 1992: Peace talks resumed as the Madrid Conference moved to Washington DC and lasted for four days.

On the same day, Hurricane Andrew, the worst natural disaster ever to hit America, produced an estimated $30 billion in damage and left 180,000 Floridians homeless. Another coincidence?

Event #3

January 16, 1994: President Bill Clinton met with the Syrian president, Hafez al-Assad, in Geneva, Switzerland. They talked about a peace agreement with Israel that would involve the Israelis giving up the Golan Heights.

Less than twenty-four hours later, a powerful earthquake with a magnitude of 6.9 on the Richter scale rocked Southern California. This quake, centered in Northridge, is the second most destructive natural disaster ever to hit the United States. It is second only to the devastation caused by Hurricane Andrew.

Event #4

Early March–April 1997: Yasser Arafat, the chairman of the Palestinian Liberation Organization (PLO) and sworn enemy of Israel, was permitted to tour the United States. The combination of his appearances in America and President Clinton rebuking Israel for the refusal to give away her land for peace coincided with some of the worst tornadoes and floods in the history of the United States.

On the very day that Arafat arrived in America, powerful tornadoes devastated broad sections of our nation, ripping across Texas, Arkansas, Mississippi, Kentucky, and Tennessee. Arafat's American tour also coincided with terrible storms in North and South Dakota that resulted in that area's worst flooding in the entire twentieth century.

It is interesting to note that as soon as Arafat finished his tour and left the United States, the storms stopped. An interesting correlation existed between these events, don't you think?

Event #5

January 21, 1998: Israel's prime minister, Benjamin Netanyahu, met with President Clinton at the White House to a chilly reception. President Clinton and Secretary of

State Madeleine Albright both refused to do so much as have lunch with him.

Shortly afterward, that same day, the Monica Lewinsky scandal exploded onto what seemed to be every media outlet on the planet and began to occupy significant portions of President Clinton's time. You sow; you reap.

Event #6

September 27 and 28, 1998: Secretary of State Albright was working on the final details of an agreement in which Israel would give up 13 percent of Yesha—a geographical area that includes Judea, Samaria, and Gaza.

That same day, Hurricane Georges slammed into the Gulf Coast and just sat there, spinning. Georges stalled out and kept blowing away, recording sustained winds of 110 mph and gusts reaching speeds of 175 mph.

On September 28, President Clinton met with Arafat and Netanyahu at the White House to finalize the land deal. Later, Arafat addressed the United Nations concerning his desire to declare an independent Palestinian state by May 1999.

While Arafat continued to speak, Hurricane Georges continued to pound the Gulf Coast, causing catastrophic damage that generated a price tag of over $1 billion. Is it a coincidence that the storm began to dissipate at the same time Arafat left the United States? I don't think so.

Event #7

October 15, 1998: Arafat and Netanyahu met at the Wye River Plantation in Maryland to continue discussions that had ended on September 28. The discussions, scheduled to last five days, focused on Israel giving up 13 percent of Yesha, and eventually carried over until October 23.

On October 17, overwhelming rains and tornadoes hit southern Texas, inundating the San Antonio area with twenty inches of rain in a twenty-four-hour period. The devastating weather continued until October 22 and eventually ravaged 25 percent of Texas. When it was all said and done, it caused over $1 billion in damage. On October 21, President Clinton declared this section of Texas a major disaster area.

Event #8

May 3, 1999: Yasser Arafat, speaking in Israel, was scheduled to declare a Palestinian state, with Jerusalem as the capital. However, the declaration was postponed to December 19, 1999, at the request of President Clinton—whose letters to Arafat were encouraging to the PLO leader's aspirations for his own land. Clinton also wrote that the Palestinians had a right to determine their future on their own land, and they deserved to live free today, tomorrow, and forever.

That same day, starting at 4:47 in the afternoon, Central Daylight Time, the most powerful tornado storm system ever to hit the United States swept across Oklahoma and Kansas. The 316-mile per hour wind-speed was the fastest ever recorded.

Event #9

August 29, 2005: Exactly one week after Israel's prime minister, Ariel Sharon, completed the forcible eviction of Jewish settlers from the Gaza Strip, Hurricane Katrina struck the states of Louisiana, Mississippi, and Alabama with a destructive and catastrophic force.

Almost the entire city of New Orleans found itself underwater. Many weather experts called Katrina the worst hurricane and natural disaster to hit the country—ever. President George W. Bush supported Sharon's evacuation of the Israelis from Gaza.

In April 2005, Bush and Sharon met in Crawford, Texas, where Bush praised Sharon for his strong visionary leadership in initiating the Gaza withdrawal, known as the Disengagement Plan. "I strongly support his courageous initiative to disengage from Gaza and part of the West Bank," he said—referring to the withdrawal of more than eight thousand Jewish settlers from Gaza.

As You Do unto Israel ...

Nine major, well-known, well-documented, and life-altering events have happened in this country directly related to our failure to stand with Israel in the land for peace negotiations. It is important to overlay the dates of one event—like George H.W. Bush's Land for Peace Initiative—together with what occurred because of it: the Perfect Storm. Look at the headlines side-by-side—this happens, and that happens; action and reaction; cause and effect.

More than ninety of these types of occurrences have happened since the land for peace discussions started. I've pointed out nine examples to you, but there are more than ten times that number. If there were only two or three incidents, there would be a case for coincidence—but not ninety. There is just too much for it all to be coincidental. Think about what God told Abraham (Abram) and his descendants in Genesis 12:

> I will bless those who bless you and curse those who curse you; and the entire world will be blessed because of you. (Genesis 12:3 TLB)

8

God's Chosen People

Satan has always wanted to divide the land of Israel because by doing so, he challenges God's Word and His covenant. Satan knows that if he can overcome God and the covenant He made with His people, he then becomes bigger than God. In fact, he becomes God. It is easy to see the conflict that goes on.

For many reasons, the Israelis have been the chosen people of God. A couple of noteworthy reasons were that our Savior and the Holy Bible came from that land. In fact, all the things that are important and sacred to us came from that area. Because of that, we do not have a right to touch that place; in fact, we are obligated to bless it and their people.

We are also God's chosen people, no question about it. Those of us in the church are the elect of God and His spiritual seed. However, the Jewish people—God's natural seed—are also God's elect. There is no conflict there at all. When you see the word *elect* in the Bible, the only way you can determine who it refers to is to establish the context in which it was written.

The Valley of Jehoshaphat

Let's look at Joel 3:2, where God says,

> I will also gather all nations, and will bring
> them down into the valley of Jehoshaphat, and
> will plead with them there for my people and
> for my heritage Israel, whom they have scattered
> among the nations, and parted my land.

Understand that there is no Valley of Jehoshaphat in Israel. It
is a type and does not exist. Likewise, you will also find that
there is a reference in scripture referring to the city of Jerusalem
as Sodom—also a type.

> I have seen also in the prophets of Jerusalem an
> horrible thing: they commit adultery, and walk in
> lies: they strengthen also the hands of evildoers,
> that none doth return from his wickedness;
> they are all of them unto me as Sodom, and
> the inhabitants thereof as Gomorrah. (Jeremiah
> 23:14)

Jerusalem and the infamous Sodom were obviously not the
same, but when God uses a type to identify something, He
does it for a reason. He is putting another name on it because
he wants to draw attention to something you would not have
otherwise seen.

So if I said to you, "Jerusalem is called Sodom," chances are you
would have an immediate association in your mind of Jerusalem
taking on the characteristics of corruption and evil that Sodom
possessed. That is as far as I am willing to go with that analogy,

as that is not the point here. However, there probably would be an immediate connection—a wicked and immoral one—that you instantly begin to associate to Jerusalem, because of the reference to Sodom.

Gathering All Nations

Referring back to the Valley of Jehoshaphat in Joel 3, there is a term that is referenced there, as well as in other places in scripture: the gathering of all nations.

> I will also gather all nations, and will bring them down into the valley of Jehoshaphat. (Joel 3:2a)

There are other references in scripture where God talks about the gathering of all nations, so God assumes that you understand what this gathering is all about. So when God refers to the Valley of Jehoshaphat, He is probably referencing all of the events related to what leads up to the gathering of the nations. In other words, the Valley of Jehoshaphat is possibly the entire region of the Middle East.

He goes on by saying,

> I will also gather all nations, and will bring them down into the valley of Jehoshaphat, and will plead with them there for my people and for my heritage Israel, whom they have scattered among the nations, and parted my land. (Joel 3:2)

All the nations are gathered together for God to make a point relating to His people, Israel. God said, "I'm going to plead with the nations there for my people and for my heritage Israel." The point is that the relationship is going to be Israel and God; God and Israel; and then everybody else.

The gathering together is a direct reference to the assembling together of different nations—at what we call Megiddo or Armageddon—for the final battle that the Lord intervenes in and ultimately stops. God said that if He did not put an end to it, no flesh would remain alive. That is how severe this thing gets.

So the Valley of Jehoshaphat could refer to all the events of the Middle East. Some scholars believe it to be that way, while others maintain that it is a reference to the Valley of Megiddo, the plain of Jezreel, or the place where this final battle takes place. Either one could be right. However, there is probably some double meaning in both.

What I want you to remember in all this is, according to scripture, all the events that push us toward Armageddon are directly related to the act of parting the land of God's chosen people, Israel. Dividing the land is a key sign that we are the rapture generation.

> And I will bless them that bless thee, and curse
> him that curseth thee. (Genesis 12:3)

God will bless those who bless Israel, and He will curse those who mean them harm. It all goes back to the parting of the land.

Let's look at Zechariah 12:2–3:

> Behold, I will make Jerusalem a cup of trembling unto all the people round about, when they shall be in the siege both against Judah and against Jerusalem.
>
> And in that day will I make Jerusalem a burdensome stone for all people: all that burden themselves with it shall be cut in pieces, though all the people of the earth be gathered together against it.

God says that the whole earth will gather against Jerusalem. Nation upon nation can try to pressure Israel to accept the two-state solution if they want to, but the wise action would be to stop interfering with them. I sure don't want to be cut into pieces. We should be praying for the peace of Israel, supporting them and showing concern for them, not meddling in their business.

"Everybody has a right to this and a right to that," you say, "but who are these people who think they can just push others around?"

Well, if you are wise, you had better control what comes out of your mouth until you learn the history behind it all. In fact, most "historical experts" don't have much of a clue what they're talking about. The earth is the Lord's and the fullness thereof, so ultimately, He has the right to give portions of it to anybody He chooses. Look at Zechariah 12:3 again:

> And in that day will I make Jerusalem a
> burdensome stone for all people: all that burden
> themselves with it shall be cut in pieces, though
> all the people of the earth be gathered together
> against it.

The gathering together is what we refer to as Armageddon. The prophetic scripture about the end times and the coming of the Lord refer to the appearing of the Lord, when Jesus comes back to the earth, and his feet touch down on the Mount of Olives. That's the time when every eye shall see Him, and everybody finally understands that Jesus is exactly who He has claimed to be all along.

A proper understanding of scripture shows us that there is a time before Jesus appears when He comes to the earth without stepping foot on the planet; I'm not talking about the birth of Jesus as a babe in a manger, either. That was His first coming. The second coming is a bit different and has a part A and a part B associated with it.

In part A, Jesus, like a thief in the night, comes for His church, and we rise to meet Him in the air. We go to heaven with Him for the Marriage Supper of the Lamb, and the twenty-one judgments begin to take place on the earth. Part B, or the second time He comes, He comes back with the church.

We are talking about the signs that lead to Armageddon. The parting of the land is a sign of His coming back to earth, but the rapture of the church happens seven years before that. If you take careful note of the news and the scripture, it makes sense that if all these references point to His appearing—physically stepping back on this earth—how much closer must the rapture of the church be?

Make no mistake about it; we are the rapture generation. You must understand that life as we know it cannot continue much longer the way it's going. It is not merely business as usual. It is not normal; it is not just a continuation of the past. We are living in different times. It is a different season, and you must be aware of the differences. All of us need to be ready to meet the Lord.

> Alas! for that day is great, so that none is like it: it is even the time of Jacob's trouble, but he shall be saved out of it. (Jeremiah 30:7)

We are living in the time of Jacob's trouble. It is not a time of the church's trouble; it is a time of Jacob's trouble. The church is raptured out, but because of the Jews' rejection of Jesus Christ, they must stay for an additional seven years.

Recognizing the End Times

To have a responsible grasp of prophetic scripture, you must first have a working understanding of the last four verses of Daniel 9. You must know and understand these verses to recognize the timeline of end-time activities.

> Seventy weeks are determined upon thy people and upon thy holy city, to finish the transgression, and to make an end of sins, and to make reconciliation for iniquity, and to bring in everlasting righteousness, and to seal up the

vision and prophecy, and to anoint the most Holy.

Know therefore and understand, that from the going forth of the commandment to restore and to build Jerusalem unto the Messiah the Prince shall be seven weeks, and threescore and two weeks: the street shall be built again, and the wall, even in troublous times.

And after threescore and two weeks shall Messiah be cut off, but not for himself: and the people of the prince that shall come shall destroy the city and the sanctuary; and the end thereof shall be with a flood, and unto the end of the war desolations are determined.

And he shall confirm the covenant with many for one week: and in the midst of the week he shall cause the sacrifice and the oblation to cease, and for the overspreading of abominations he shall make it desolate, even until the consummation, and that determined shall be poured upon the desolate. (Daniel 9:24–27)

Let me explain: There are sixty-nine weeks in the books, but there is a seventieth week coming that is God's time of dealing with the Jews. However, between week sixty-nine and seventy is a two-thousand-year period called the church age. God has dealt with the Jews for sixty-nine weeks, but He has one more to go. All Israel shall be saved, scripture says, but blindness has happened to the Jews, in part, so that the Gentiles may be saved and come to God. Let's look at Romans 11 in a couple of different versions:

> For I would not, brethren, that ye should be ignorant of this mystery, lest ye should be wise in your own conceits; that blindness in part is happened to Israel, until the fulness of the Gentiles be come in. (Romans 11:25 KJV)

> I want you to understand this secret truth, brothers and sisters. This truth will help you understand that you don't know everything. The truth is this: Part of Israel has been made stubborn, but that will change when enough non-Jewish people have come to God. (Romans 11:25 ERV)

Jerusalem will be trodden down by the Gentiles until the time of the Gentiles is fulfilled. We live in the time of the Gentiles, but it is ending. We are coming to the end of the church age and into the beginning of the Tribulation period, or the time of Jacob's trouble. It is a time of God's wrath upon the earth. Remember, however, that God has not appointed us to wrath but to receive salvation and redemption from Him. We are not here during that period because we are in heaven. The Jews are then going to find their Messiah, as God brings them back to Him both physically and spiritually.

When we hear these things, we know they are true because the Bible establishes it. I'm not trying to wrestle the scripture to come up with some political position; I'm just being honest with scripture.

Some Final Thoughts

We have a church in this country that is asleep at the wheel. We don't see what's right in front of us. But if you pay attention to the information in this book, you will not be left in the dark.

This book may bother you because of the truth it represents. But that's okay; just stay the course. Being troubled or anxious because of the truth is just another sign of the end times.

"I don't want to hear this," you say. "It bothers me."

It ought to bother you, but you cannot ignore it because ignoring it will not change the reality of it—not even a little.

But just what does this mean to you and me today? First off, we need to be ready to meet Jesus. We need to make sure that our spiritual life is in proper order—that we have received Jesus as our Lord and Savior, and we are living like He would want us to. We also need to make sure that—as much as is possible—everybody around us is also ready. We need to be more evangelistic; we don't have the luxury of time that we had in the past. Time on this planet is running out.

9

Alignment of the Prophetic Nations

You should be becoming more aware of how current world events relate to the rapture of the church. Circumstances are different now, but you are gaining confidence because you are becoming more knowledgeable and are no longer in the dark. That's a good thing.

The Fig Tree and the Nation of Israel

> Now learn a parable of the fig tree; When his branch is yet tender, and putteth forth leaves, ye know that summer is nigh:
>
> So likewise ye, when ye shall see all these things, know that it is near, even at the doors.
>
> Verily I say unto you, This generation shall not pass, till all these things be fulfilled. (Matthew 24:32–34)

Jesus said that when you see the fig tree bud, you will know that the process that starts the progression toward the rapture has begun. Once you see the fig tree bud, not a generation will pass till everything is fulfilled. Scripture tells us that the fig tree is the nation of Israel. In addition to finding that in the books of Joel and Hosea, Jesus made similar statements that the fig tree is the sign that we are *the* generation.

"I just don't believe that the fig tree is Israel," you say.

I won't argue with you, but I must disagree. The reason I do believe it is because everything we're talking about here is found in other places where the fig tree isn't even mentioned. The context of the fig tree and all the things related to it are validated in different books of the Bible. That's important because we interpret scripture with scripture. The fig tree is our sign that we are the generation.

Luke recorded this parable a little differently than Matthew did. Luke 21:29–33 says this:

> And he spake to them a parable; Behold the fig tree, and all the trees;
>
> When they now shoot forth, ye see and know of your own selves that summer is now nigh at hand.
>
> So likewise ye, when ye see these things come to pass, know ye that the kingdom of God is nigh at hand.

> Verily I say unto you, This generation shall not
> pass away, till all be fulfilled.
>
> Heaven and earth shall pass away: but my words
> shall not pass away.

The Fig Tree versus All the Trees

The point I want to make from Luke 21 comes from verse 29:

> Behold the fig tree, and all the trees.

According to the book of Joel and other places, trees represent nations. So when we see the fig tree referenced in scripture, we can be confident that they are talking about Israel. When the phrase "all the trees" or "any other tree" shows up, Jesus is referring to other prophetic nations.

Several nations mentioned in the Bible have tremendous prophetic significance, while others have little to none. God loves all these nations and the people living in them, but they are not players in the end-times conversation. They are not chess pieces on the board. They exist, they are important, God loves them, and they all need evangelism, but they are not players.

The players are the prophetic nations mentioned in scripture. Babylon, which is today located in Iraq, is mentioned more than any other nation except Israel. With that said, do you think Babylon would have any significance in the end-times conversation? Babylon is a prophetic nation. It plays a significant role in what's going on in the world today.

In the book of Revelation, the Bible talks about the destruction of Mystery Babylon. Is it talking about the Babylon of the Middle East? Probably not. It is, in fact, a type that refers to a Babylonian system following the example set in place by the original Babylon. I am saying this so you know these nations are extremely relevant. Remember, Israel is represented by the fig tree, while other trees mentioned are prophetic nations of a somewhat lesser degree.

The Enemies of God

Look at Psalm 83:1–2a, and you can begin to find some of the prophetic nations mentioned in this passage.

> Keep not thou silence, O God: hold not thy peace, and be not still, O God.
>
> For, lo, thine enemies make a tumult.

These people are the enemies of God and enemies of the things of God. If they are enemies of the God of the Bible, it may not be politically correct, but they are your enemies too. We need to wise up.

> For, lo, thine enemies make a tumult: and they that hate thee have lifted up the head.
>
> They have taken crafty counsel against thy people, and consulted against thy hidden ones. (Psalm 83:2–3)

These people are your enemies as well as enemies of the church and the nation of Israel.

> They have said, Come, and let us cut them off from being a nation; that the name of Israel may be no more in remembrance. (Psalm 83:4)

Here is verse 4 from the New Living Translation:

> "Come," they say, "let us wipe out Israel as a nation. We will destroy the very memory of its existence."

These are the enemies of God and the nation of Israel that want to wipe God's people from the face of the earth. They want to annihilate them. They want to destroy them to the point where people will not even remember that the nation of Israel ever existed.

It's Happening Now

Thinking like that has existed down through history, but it's different this time. Because we are the rapture generation, these events are wrapped around an event that is strategically important—extremely important for the time in which we are living.

10

THERE IS A WAR COMING

For they have consulted together with one consent: they are confederate against thee. (Psalm 83:5)

A confederation or alliance was established at a particular time in history in the unfolding of prophetic events. There is a confederation of specific groups of people who stand against Israel, against God, and against the people of God. They stand against Israel and everything you stand for. They are against the people of God.

If you are a person of God, you need to identify yourself so you know which side of the fence you're on. Don't hesitate; identify yourself. I am, without apology, a Christian and a follower of Christ. I am not going to change and do something else. I am not going to blend. I am standing fast. My advice: don't end up on the wrong side of this one.

Some things in this politically correct world bother me more than others. However, as a minister, I am here to comfort the afflicted and afflict the comfortable. Because we don't want to offend people, we tend to shy away from saying anything controversial. So upfront, I'm going to tell you in no uncertain terms, I could do it. I could bother you. In fact, I might even try to make you uncomfortable on purpose. So if I turn over one or two of your sacred cows, don't be shocked. It's coming.

"But God wants me to be happy, right?" you exclaim.

Wrong. God wants you to be right. If you can be happy and be right, that's okay, but if you have to choose between being right and being happy; being right is more important.

What Is a Confederacy?

A good definition of a confederacy is a league or covenant between a group of people. It's an alliance between persons, parties, or states for some purpose. With that in mind, as you do your research and analyze what you are seeing, you will inevitably come to places where you notice the Tabernacles of Edom.

The Tabernacles of Edom

A good, modern-day illustration of the Tabernacles of Edom—Edomites being one of the enemies of God—could be likened to the tents of the refugees in Jordan. These are the tents of Edom, and they exist today. Those refugee tents—the Tabernacles, or the tents of Edom—are their world, and even their people will not let them cease to be refugees because of the political importance their refugee status is to their political position. The images of them are the photo ops to the world.

The media can make a group of people look especially guilty for what they have done when, in reality, other people are actually to blame. There are strategies at work here, like shooting rockets all day long from weapon emplacements in elementary schools. Because of the location of their weapons, Israel can't effectively retaliate because of the potential loss of innocent, young lives. You understand?

The tabernacles of Edom exist today, inhabited by an actual group of people. Their description is revealed in Psalm 83:5–12 (emphasis added):

> For they have consulted together with one consent: they are confederate against thee:
>
> **The tabernacles of Edom**, and the Ishmaelites; of Moab, and the Hagarenes;
>
> Gebal, and Ammon, and Amalek; the Philistines with the inhabitants of Tyre;
>
> Assur also is joined with them: they have holpen the children of Lot. Selah.
>
> Do unto them as unto the Midianites; as to Sisera, as to Jabin, at the brook of Kison:
>
> Which perished at Endor: they became as dung for the earth.
>
> Make their nobles like Oreb, and like Zeeb: yea, all their princes as Zebah, and as Zalmunna:

Who said, Let us take to ourselves the houses
of God in possession.

In verse 7, the word *Ammon* appears. Ammon is a city in Jordan whose origins, along with a few others mentioned, can't be identified with their current geography. The nations, as we know them today, do not have the same boundaries from when they first existed, so they have to be identified by people groups rather than real estate. However, you can decipher and deduce who the nations are if you analyze them carefully.

Looking further down the verse and into the next, we see the Philistines and the inhabitants of Tyre, a city in Lebanon. Other players are Egypt, Syria, Jordan, Iraq, Gaza, and the Palestinians. They are all mentioned in that passage.

The Bible says that the confederation that will come against Israel—that calls God their enemy—is the group just listed, containing Egypt and Syria among others. Keep that in mind as you watch the news every day.

Syria

Syria is in the throes of civil war. Bashar al-Assad—Syria's president, commander-in-chief of the Syrian Armed Forces, general secretary of the ruling Ba'ath Party, and regional secretary of the party's branch in Syria—used weapons of mass destruction (including poisonous gas) on his own people.

The Islamic State of Iraq and Syria (ISIS), also called the Islamic State of Iraq and the Levant (ISIL), is working very hard to establish and maintain a strong presence in Syria. The chess pieces—the nations you hear about in the news every day—are on the table now.

Jordan

A Jordanian pilot was killed, and they were in the news a while back for the bombing of some ISIS targets.

Iraq

Iraq is in the news all the time. ISIS wants to take Iraq and form a caliphate, a powerful and cohesive organization with a great desire to become an established Islamic state rather than just a radical group. In this case, the caliphate wants to become a nation that rallies together all the factions in the region for the common cause to destroy Israel and rule the world. Make no mistake; ISIS is after the destruction of Israel, and a caliphate only makes them stronger.

Gaza

Israel had to invade Gaza sometime back because of all the concrete, steel, and other things they brought in to help them rebuild and strengthen their wartime infrastructure. They built rocket emplacements in underground tunnels—and the use of concrete and reinforced steel would help them do that. It would pose an even bigger problem for Israel.

The Nations Are in Play

These nations are in play. They are pieces on the chessboard of world events. These reasons, among other things, lead me to believe that we are the rapture generation.

Good Guys Win, Bad Guys Lose

There is good news in all this, however, and it is twofold:

1. We are not going to go through this conflict.
2. The radicals will lose.

As it says in Psalm 83:12 and continuing through the end of the chapter, there is clearly a conflict, but the enemies of God lose everything. Israel doesn't.

> Who said, Let us take to ourselves the houses of God in possession.
>
> O my God, make them like a wheel; as the stubble before the wind.
>
> As the fire burneth a wood, and as the flame setteth the mountains on fire;
>
> So persecute them with thy tempest, and make them afraid with thy storm.
>
> Fill their faces with shame; that they may seek thy name, O Lord.

Let them be confounded and troubled for ever;
yea, let them be put to shame, and perish:

That men may know that thou, whose name
alone is Jehovah, art the most high over all the
earth. (Psalm 83:12–18)

So there will evidently be an escalation of force, resulting in a military confrontation with Israel's immediate neighbors—those closest to its borders. That is important because the next onfederacy or people group that you deal with comes at a time when Israel is at peace with its neighbors.

These nations exist, are in play, and none are on the sidelines. Countries like Brazil, Argentina, and Chile, in contrast, are not prophetic nations. They are important because God loves them and loves the people who live there. Although they do not show up as prophetic nations, we should never minimize them in any way. They represent the "other trees" that Jesus spoke of when He referred to the fig tree and the other trees. However, they do not have a stake in the game to the degree that the prophetic nations do.

You can be confident in knowing that when you see these signs, not a generation will pass until the end-time prophecy is fulfilled. All of it. This thing is wrapping up. That is exactly what Jesus said.

Obadiah's Vision

So we have this event described in Psalm 83, which is also mentioned in the book of Obadiah. I believe it gives us more detail of what the Psalm 83 battle is all about. Let's take a look at it:

> The vision of Obadiah. Thus saith the Lord God concerning Edom; We have heard a rumour from the Lord, and an ambassador is sent among the heathen, Arise ye, and let us rise up against her in battle.
>
> Behold, I have made thee small among the heathen: thou art greatly despised.
>
> The pride of thine heart hath deceived thee, thou that dwellest in the clefts of the rock, whose habitation is high; that saith in his heart, Who shall bring me down to the ground?
>
> Though thou exalt thyself as the eagle, and though thou set thy nest among the stars, thence will I bring thee down, saith the Lord.
>
> If thieves came to thee, if robbers by night, (how art thou cut off!) would they not have stolen till they had enough? if the grapegatherers came to thee, would they not leave some grapes?
>
> How are the things of Esau searched out! how are his hidden things sought up!
>
> All the men of thy confederacy have brought thee even to the border: the men that were at peace with thee have deceived thee, and prevailed against thee; they that eat thy bread

have laid a wound under thee: there is none understanding in him.

Shall I not in that day, saith the Lord, even destroy the wise men out of Edom, and understanding out of the mount of Esau?

And thy mighty men, O Teman, shall be dismayed, to the end that every one of the mount of Esau may be cut off by slaughter.

For thy violence against thy brother Jacob shame shall cover thee, and thou shalt be cut off for ever.

In the day that thou stoodest on the other side, in the day that the strangers carried away captive his forces, and foreigners entered into his gates, and cast lots upon Jerusalem, even thou wast as one of them.

But thou shouldest not have looked on the day of thy brother in the day that he became a stranger; neither shouldest thou have rejoiced over the children of Judah in the day of their destruction; neither shouldest thou have spoken proudly in the day of distress.

Thou shouldest not have entered into the gate of my people in the day of their calamity; yea, thou shouldest not have looked on their affliction in the day of their calamity, nor have laid hands on their substance in the day of their calamity;

Neither shouldest thou have stood in the crossway, to cut off those of his that did escape; neither shouldest thou have delivered up those of his that did remain in the day of distress.

For the day of the Lord is near upon all the heathen: as thou hast done, it shall be done unto thee: thy reward shall return upon thine own head.

For as ye have drunk upon my holy mountain, so shall all the heathen drink continually, yea, they shall drink, and they shall swallow down, and they shall be as though they had not been.

But upon mount Zion shall be deliverance, and there shall be holiness; and the house of Jacob shall possess their possessions.

And the house of Jacob shall be a fire, and the house of Joseph a flame, and the house of Esau for stubble, and they shall kindle in them, and devour them; and there shall not be any remaining of the house of Esau; for the Lord hath spoken it.

And they of the south shall possess the mount of Esau; and they of the plain the Philistines: and they shall possess the fields of Ephraim, and the fields of Samaria: and Benjamin shall possess Gilead.

And the captivity of this host of the children of Israel shall possess that of the Canaanites, even unto Zarephath; and the captivity of Jerusalem, which is in Sepharad, shall possess the cities of the south.

And saviours shall come up on mount Zion to judge the mount of Esau; and the kingdom shall be the Lord's. (Obadiah 1–21)

In Ezekiel 38, we have something that is similar but different from Psalm 83. Some people just lump it all together and say, "It's all the same event." But no, it's not. It is distinctly different. The people groups mentioned there are different; therefore, you know they cannot be the same.

And the word of the Lord came unto me, saying, Son of man, set thy face against Gog, the land of Magog, the chief prince of Meshech and Tubal, and prophesy against him. (Ezekiel 38:1–2)

Let's read the second verse from the Amplified Bible:

Son of man, set your face against Gog, of the land of Magog, **the prince of Rosh**, of Meshech, and of Tubal, and prophesy against him. (Ezekiel 38:2 AMP, emphasis added)

Let's Not Forget Russia

The word that I want you to pay close attention to is "Rosh." It is found in Ezekiel 38:2, in the Amplified Bible, and is another word for Russia. So now you know that when the Bible speaks of Rosh, it is talking about Russia. Subsequently, we find that God says that this coalition is not the tents of Edom, but it starts in Russia:

> And say, Thus saith the Lord God; Behold, I am against thee, O Gog, the chief prince of Meshech and Tubal. (Ezekiel 38:3)

When Ezekiel speaks of Meshech and Tubal, he is talking about what is now Moscow and Tobolsk.

> And I will turn thee back, and put hooks into thy jaws, and I will bring thee forth, and all thine army, horses and horsemen, all of them clothed with all sorts of armour, even a great company with bucklers and shields, all of them handling swords. (Ezekiel 38:3–4)

Notice that when the Bible gives you an order, it places the most important thing first; then the second in importance, then third, fourth, and so on. It gives you an order of descending importance. With that in mind, Russia has the top spot, and the next is Persia.

> Persia, Ethiopia, and Libya with them; all of them with shield and helmet:

Gomer, and all his bands; the house of Togarmah
of the north quarters, and all his bands: and
many people with thee. (Ezekiel 38:5)

Here is another confederacy—or another coalition—led by
Russia, with an Islamic following. Every single one of these
nations are Islamic. Russia does some things in advancement
toward Israel with an Islamic confederacy and an Islamic
coalition, with the second most important one of the group
being Persia.

In 1935, Persia became Iran, and in the process, Russia and
Iran have become the key players in this event. It sounds like
something you would hear on today's news, doesn't it? That is
another reason why I believe that we are the rapture generation.

To reiterate, in order of importance, God says that Russia comes
in first, and then Iran. Coming in third is …

Libya

The deposed Libyan leader Muammar Gaddafi was killed in
2011, which cleared the path for ISIS to begin its quest for a
takeover of the country. They have been in a governmental
reformation, with chaos the order of the day.

How about the Benghazi incident? Some call it a scandal,
while others write it off to a lack of news. We've never received
a satisfactory explanation of why our ambassador to Libya and
others were attacked and murdered on September 11, 2012.
Then, in 2015, two senior leaders of ISIL were killed in Libya.
US military interdiction succeeded in ending ISIS control over

substantial territory in Libya in 2016. In September of 2017, the Trump administration suspended certain Libyan nationals—along with those from Iran, Libya, Somalia, Sudan, Syria, and Yemen—from entering the United States.

Libya is in the middle of the northernmost part of the African continent. When you read about Libya in this passage, we are talking about people groups in the borders of that day. In biblical times, Libya included Tunisia and Algeria. Remember, the boundaries are different today. Then we have …

Ethiopia

Also in this list is Ethiopia, or Cush, as it was known then. In biblical times, when you reference Ethiopia, you have to include Sudan and Somalia. There have been more people killed for their faith in Sudan than maybe any other place on the planet—and it is spreading. One of the most notable Christian persecutions of the last century happened in Sudan, a country that has not had a government in over twenty years. They, too, are players in the news today.

You may remember *Captain Phillips*, a movie that came out in 2013. It was a true story about Capt. Richard Phillips (played by Tom Hanks), the captain of a container ship that was hijacked in 2009. The pirates who seized the ship originated from Somalia.

Many Somali refugees made their way to the northernmost parts of the United States. It was all over the news when authorities discovered a terrorist plot that involved the Mall of America in Minneapolis, Minnesota. That plan was formulated by some Somali refugees who wanted to destroy the mall and everyone inside it. Just another reason why I believe that we are "the" generation.

Some people may believe that these activities have been going on forever. They say, "It's just life; it's just the norm." I don't agree at all. Life is different today in so many ways. We are living in a time that is not even close to being normal.

Persia

Persia and Libya—Cush and Put, in some translations—were the homes of offspring of Noah and others. At one time, the Persian Empire was one of the largest empires in history, ruling nearly 50 percent of the world's population and consuming approximately 2.1 million square miles. Today, Persia is known primarily as the country of Iran. These are the people groups. You have to discount the current boundaries, since they did not exist at that time.

Turkey

Today, Gomer is primarily Turkey. Turkey is located directly to the north of Iraq and immediately to the south of Russia. The scripture says that Israel's enemies will come out of the north quarters. Here's what the book of Ezekiel has to say about the account:

> After many days thou shalt be visited: in the latter years thou shalt come into the land that is brought back from the sword, and is gathered

out of many people [that is a reference to Israel coming back to its land] against the mountains of Israel, which have been always waste: but it is brought forth out of the nations, and they shall dwell safely all of them.

Thou shalt ascend and come like a storm, thou shalt be like a cloud to cover the land, thou, and all thy bands, and many people with thee. (Ezekiel 38:8–9)

The storm spoken of in verse 9 is a blitzkrieg-type of attack: a sudden, secret attack, a massive assault without warning. It is essential for you to understand that the nations we are talking about are all in play today. None of them are sitting on the sidelines. It is a hotbed of ongoing activity.

We sold $80 billion worth of weapons to Saudi Arabia to help them in their defensive efforts. Now, the Saudis are talking very seriously about going nuclear because they fear that Iran is well on their way to doing the same.

Yemen

During the Obama administration, Yemen was called a policy success story in the Middle East. However, the Yemeni government fell, and Saudi Arabia started bombing them. I guess we have different definitions of success. If destabilization was the goal, then we were very successful.

Tunisia

Do you remember the Arab Spring? This was a series of protests and demonstrations across the Middle East and North Africa, with the aim of destabilizing the region and overthrowing those in power. After the government of Egypt became destabilized, President Hosni Mubarak was taken out of power. The result was the destabilization of Jordan. Libya was destabilized because of the Arab Spring, and it all started in Tunisia. They are all in play. Remember, Jesus said, "Watch the trees." When you see the wind blowing through the leaves of these trees, you had better wake up. Something is going on.

You Must Pay Attention

You have choices. You can stick your head in every electronic mobile device you own, liking and following everybody. "I like you. Do you like me?" Oh, brother. You could also become absorbed in video games or consumed by Netflix, Hulu, or whatever the latest craze is that's holding everyone's attention. That is all well and good, but what you need to do instead is spend some quality time paying attention to what's going on in the world around you. You better pay attention because that is what is real and relevant.

We tend to approach life in a very deceptive way. We don't even believe half of what we see anymore. We've become absorbed in video games and movies—Captain America or some other fake, Superman-type hero. The problem is, "Ain't no superhero gonna stop these end-time events, honey." The end is coming, and the generation that sees it start will watch it finish. Not my words; those words come straight from the Bible.

You can say, "Well, I don't know if that's what's really going on."

Play it that way if you must, but we only have one pass at life, so I'm going to take advantage of the one I have. I believe it is *the* event, and I believe we are in it.

The Scripture Sounds Like Today's News

Again, Russia and Iran are the two most important nations from those previously mentioned. They are the leaders of the confederacy (not that the others are unimportant, but they are "the other trees"). Did you find it as sobering as I did when you realized just how similar the scripture and today's news are?

Rebuffing NATO

When Jens Stoltenberg, the secretary-general of NATO, was in the United States in 2015, President Obama decided—despite repeated requests—not to meet with him. That was a huge mistake. Not giving NATO an audience was a failure to secure that particular region, which is what led to the Russian invasion of Ukraine.

Russia started negotiating with Cuba, Honduras, and Venezuela to establish military bases with rockets capable of reaching the mainland of the United States. So what did we do? Nothing. In fact, our actions were tantamount to saying, "Bring it on."

Iran was then (and is now) attempting to go nuclear, and all we could say was, "Well, you guys just negotiate for the right to do it." Negotiate for the right to do it? We are talking about Iran, for crying out loud.

"It's a good deal for us," our leaders said.

Amazing. If I had not seen it with my own two eyes, I would not have believed it—but I did see it. We have lost our way.

Is a Weak US Necessary?

Many prophetic Bible teachers believe—not just because of these events but because they have seen what has been happening in our country—that a weakened United States would be necessary to encourage these nations to come forward. We saw it with the failing foreign policy and politically hamstrung military of the Obama administration. It emboldened the enemies of God, the enemies of the Bible, the enemies of the church, the enemies of Israel, and the enemies of our nation.

Other countries by themselves are not a deterrent, but we emboldened them to come forward and put no restraint on them whatsoever. The United States should have been counted on to offer help, but we failed miserably. Only now, in the Trump administration, are we beginning to see things change.

Get Serious

Please stop your preoccupation with your Facebook and Twitter accounts and all the other things in your life that are designed to distract you from reality. "If I like you, will you like me?

I'll follow you if you follow me." Please. There are vastly more important events going on, and we need to be aware of them.

"Please don't unlike me."

No Respect

Under the Obama administration, Russia laughed at the United States. Today, Iran carries on with the development of its nuclear capability, and North Korea is creating a nuclear footprint. While Iran negotiates with us on the one hand, their ayatollah is declaring, "Death to America," on the other. The politicians of the Obama administration and Hillary Clinton, in particular, had the audacity to tell us what a great deal they were negotiating. After all, the Iranians surely do not want to kill us, they said. We believed that we could negotiate a deal.

Where did our common sense go?

Russia operates militarily in Iraq and started moving additional warships toward Yemen. They wanted to intrude in Saudi Arabia, which makes the Saudis desire a nuclear option for their country. We have had to send warships to escort our ships in and out of the region because of the unrest.

I would be remiss if I did not tell you that there are competent, God-fearing Bible scholars who come down on either side of the battle of Gog and Magog. Some of them believe that this battle happens just before the rapture of the church, while others believe it happens just after. However, all Bible scholars of our persuasion—who believe in a pre-millennial, pre-Tribulation rapture—are convinced that the rapture of the church and the battle of Gog and Magog happen virtually simultaneously. Regardless of their views, they all believe they are connected. I believe that the battle of Gog and Magog happens after the rapture of the church. One reason is found in Ezekiel 38:18–19:

> And it shall come to pass at the same time when Gog shall come against the land of Israel, saith the Lord God, that my fury shall come up in my face.
>
> For in my jealousy and in the fire of my wrath have I spoken, Surely in that day there shall be a great shaking in the land of Israel.

God's Wrath Is Bypassed

Notice the word *wrath*. God doesn't just stick some random word in a verse to fill space. When God uses a word, it is there for a reason. We know that the Tribulation period is a time of God's wrath on earth. But remember that the Bible also says that we, the born-again believers, have not been appointed unto wrath. You will find that in a number of places through the Bible. Let's break it down:

- If the Tribulation period is a time for wrath, and
- we've not been appointed unto wrath, then
- the church is not here for the wrath of the Tribulation.

When Is It?

Since the Tribulation is a time of God's wrath, I happen to believe that the rapture of the church occurs just before it starts.

We haven't been chosen to go through it. That's logical, don't you think?

Do you believe that Russia is heathen from top to bottom and side to side, or are there born-again people living there? There are, in fact, many people in Russia who love the Lord. Do you believe God loves the Russian people? Of course, He does. Do you think God loves them any more than He loves you? Does He love you any more than He loves them? Are you more entitled to freedom than they are? Are they not just as entitled to escape as you are?

We know when this battle takes place too. You can find it in Ezekiel 39:1–2a:

> Therefore, thou son of man, prophesy against Gog, and say, Thus saith the Lord God; Behold, I am against thee, O Gog, the chief prince of Meshech and Tubal:
>
> And I will turn thee back, and leave but the sixth part of thee.

Five-sixths of the Russian people who have anything to do with this event are slaughtered. Five of every six people involved in this battle will die. That is over 83 percent of them. You may say, "God loves the Russian Christians as much as He loves us, right? He is just as obligated to them as He is to us, isn't He? I don't believe that God would do that to them. I don't think that 83 percent of the people would die before the rapture of the church. I just can't believe that. I believe they're just as entitled to escape as we are."

A Big War Is Coming

I hear what you're saying. However, there is a war coming—a big one. Russia and Iran—who are enemies of Israel—are going to push it. The United States, on the other hand, is probably going to sit on the sidelines. That means that they are opposed to the invasion, but they do nothing about it. That could be because they are passive and don't want to participate, or because it happened so quickly that they don't have time to respond. You can find that in Ezekiel 38:12–13 (emphasis added):

> To take a spoil, and to take a prey; to turn thine hand upon the desolate places that are now inhabited, and upon the people that are gathered out of the nations, which have gotten cattle and goods, that dwell in the midst of the land.
>
> **Sheba, and Dedan, and the merchants of Tarshish, with all the young lions thereof,** shall say unto thee, Art thou come to take a spoil? hast thou gathered thy company to take a prey? to carry away silver and gold, to take away cattle and goods, to take a great spoil?

Sheba and Dedan are modern-day Saudi Arabia. The young lions mentioned here are the offspring of Great Britain. Great Britain is the lion, and her offspring is the United States, New Zealand, South Africa, and others. They all sit on the sidelines when this attack happens and fail to defend Israel. The prevailing passive attitude of these countries emboldens Russia to charge into battle.

I want you to notice the fact that we are not engaged in the process. The United States, supposedly the keepers of peace in the world, have allowed the balance of powers to shift, the shift occurring because of the policies of the Obama administration.

The battle of Gog and Magog is the beginning of the battle that, without ceasing, takes the world toward Armageddon. Once that happens, once the Tribulation begins, it goes on for seven years—exactly seven years. The Bible even breaks it down to the number of days. The war does not last for seven years and six months, nor seven years and two days, but seven years to the day. So once it starts, it's a one-way trip to Armageddon. Gog and Magog light the fuse.

Why do I believe that we are the rapture generation? Look at what Jesus said:

> And ye shall hear of wars and rumours of wars: see that ye be not troubled: for all these things must come to pass, but the end is not yet.

> For nation shall rise against nation, and kingdom against kingdom: and there shall be famines, and pestilences, and earthquakes, in divers places. (Matthew 24:6–7)

11

WE ARE THE RAPTURE GENERATION

There are wars, rumors of wars, and earthquakes—absolute specifics—all signs of the end times. You may not want to think about these things, but failure to think about the end times won't change anything. It is coming, and it is better to think about it now, while you can still do something about your situation. You need to be ready.

The Twenty-One Judgments

There are twenty-one judgments mentioned during the Tribulation. They start in Revelation 6 and continue through chapter 16. Some of them look the same or at least very similar, but if you notice how they are written, even though it may be the same judgment with the same outgrowth and description, it increases in intensity as it goes along.

There are three categories of judgments: the Seal Judgments, Trumpet Judgments, and Vial Judgments. There are also seven judgments in each category.

The Seal Judgments are the first category, found in Revelation 6:1–17 and 8:1.

- The first judgment is the White Horse Rider (the antichrist).
- Then comes the Red Horse Rider (War).
- The Black Horse Rider (Famine) comes next.
- Then the Pale Horse Rider (Death) shows up.
- The martyring of believers follows them.
- Then the earthquakes come—causing the sun to turn black and the moon to be as blood; the stars fall from the heavens, causing men to hide among the rocks of the mountains, pleading for the mass of rock and stone to fall on them.
- Finally, total silence in the heavens ensues for about an hour and produces an enormous level of fear of what is to come.

The Trumpet Judgments are the second category found in Revelation chapters 8, 9, and 11.

- The first judgment here contains hail, fire, and blood; the third part of the trees and all the green grass burn up.
- Then the oceans catch on fire, turning a third of them to blood, killing a third of the living sea creatures, and destroying a third of the ships.
- Next, a third of the lakes and rivers catch on fire and become bitter, killing many men.
- Then, a third of the sun, moon, and stars go dark.
- An invasion of locusts—as powerful as scorpions—torments men to the point where they want to die.

- Then, the world's greatest army of two hundred million men kills a third of all mankind.
- The world's greatest storm then materializes; it includes lightning, thunder, a great hailstorm, and a mighty earthquake.

Finally, the Vial (or Bowl) Judgments make their appearance. You can reference all of them in Revelation 16.

- Horrible, malignant sores show up on everyone who has the mark of the beast.
- The seas become as the blood of a corpse, and every living thing dies there.
- The rivers and springs turn to blood.
- The sun scorches everyone with its fire.
- Everyone is plunged into total darkness.
- The Euphrates River dries up so that the kings from the east can march their armies toward the west without hindrance.
- The greatest earthquake since time began strikes the earth with such power that cities of many nations are reduced to piles of rubble. Every island disappears into the oceans, and the mountains are all leveled. A terrible storm with hailstones weighing as much as seventy-five pounds pummel the people below.

Russia and Iran Start the Conflict

> I will also gather all nations, and will bring them down into the valley of Jehoshaphat, and will plead with them there for my people and for my heritage Israel, whom they have

scattered among the nations, and parted my land. (Joel 3:2)

The parting and the dividing of the land—the two-state solution that is being pushed on everybody—is the reason that God judges the nations. It is the reason that this process of Armageddon starts. It's the parting of the land, with Russia and Iran being the key players that we see right now.

"What if it's somebody else?" you may ask.

It could be, but it's not. It was prophesied a great many centuries ago. I didn't get up this morning and write it down on a napkin. This was put in play by the prophets thousands of years ago as they told us what was coming and exactly what was going to happen.

The Kings of the East

Let me make one more reference here, although it is not as direct as these others I've shown you. Revelation 16:12 refers to the kings of the east:

> And the sixth angel poured out his vial upon the great river Euphrates; and the water thereof was dried up, that the way of the kings of the east might be prepared.

Let's look at Revelation 9:15:

> And the four angels were loosed, which were prepared for an hour, and a day, and a month, and a year, for to slay the third part of men.

Notice the time. We'll look at it in reverse order, so it will be less confusing: One year (twelve months) + one month + one day (twenty-five hours) + one hour. All that works out to thirteen months + twenty-five hours: an hour, a day, a month, and a year.

Let me explain what's going on here. After the sixth angel pours out his vial, the Euphrates River dries up, and the kings of the east march across.

> And the sixth angel poured out his vial upon the great river Euphrates; and the water thereof was dried up, that the way of the kings of the east might be prepared. (Revelation 16:12)

During their march toward Israel, they destroy one-third of the population of the human race—33 percent of all humankind. That's during the Tribulation. Then they come to Jerusalem. Jeremiah 3:17 says all nations shall be gathered at Jerusalem. Let's look at the first part of the verse:

> At that time they shall call Jerusalem the throne of the Lord; and **all** the **nations shall be gathered** unto it. (Jeremiah 3:17a, emphasis added)

These kings of the east—primarily China and other Asian nations—comprise the two-hundred-million-man army marching toward Israel. That little hike takes thirteen months, one day, and one hour. Exactly. For that reason, China is not a player until approximately the last year of the Tribulation period. However, a strong China is prophesied—both economically and militarily. They have to be a player. China is not the instigator of this conflict—Russia is—but they are the finishers.

The idea here is not to look at China as the sign; look at Russia. China has a thirteen-month window, and then it closes. China has to be strong militarily and economically.

When You See These Things

Jesus told us in Luke 21:31:

> So likewise ye, when ye see these things come to pass, know ye that the kingdom of God is nigh at hand.

Jesus said that when you start seeing these things, you're close to the end. Very close.

Because of these things I've been telling you, I believe that we are the rapture generation, and I offer no apologies for saying it. I'm not talking about ambiguous, unclear things, but rather about things you cannot possibly miss. I'm not talking in vague concepts; I'm talking about clear, distinct absolutes. God's Word is coming to pass right before our eyes, and I'm going to impart several truths to you in this book so you'll be more informed than most.

> And when these things begin to come to pass, then look up, and lift up your heads; for your redemption draweth nigh. (Luke 21:28)

Notice that Jesus said that your redemption draws near when these signs begin to appear, not after they have already occurred. He said that when you start to see them, get ready because He is coming for you. Be ready, and be prepared, because we are getting out of here. We're leaving.

> Watch ye therefore, and pray always, that ye may be accounted worthy to escape all these things that shall come to pass, and to stand before the Son of man. (Luke 21:36)

Jesus is showing us an escape hatch, so we need to follow His directions. We have to be ready. We have to be worthy. The obvious question on your lips is probably, "That's all well and good, but what do we have to do to be worthy?" Scripture says:

> For the Lord himself shall descend from heaven with a shout, with the voice of the archangel, and with the trump of God: and the dead in Christ shall rise first:
>
> Then we which are alive and remain shall be caught up together with them in the clouds, to meet the Lord in the air: and so shall we ever be with the Lord."
>
> Wherefore comfort one another with these words. (1 Thessalonians 4:16–18)

Jesus did not say to scare the daylights out of each other with these words; He said to comfort one other with them. In fact, the only reason that we should be afraid is if we were not ready to meet the Lord. That is the only reason. So what do you do to get ready? The answer lies in scripture. It says:

> For the Lord himself shall descend from heaven with a shout, with the voice of the archangel, and with the trump of God: and **the dead in Christ shall rise first**. (1 Thessalonians 4:16, emphasis added)

You get ready by being in Christ. But how do you do that? It's as simple as praying a simple prayer. Just talk to the Lord and say, "Jesus, I take you right now, as my Lord and my Savior. Come into me, come into my heart, and forgive me of my sins. Cleanse me by Your blood." That's it. Now you are in Christ.

Your good works will not make you worthy. Perfection will not do it, either. It is impossible to do everything correctly. You are worthy because Jesus is worthy. You're in because He's in. God does not judge us based on how good we are; He judges us based on the blood of Christ applied to our lives. Jesus forgives all of us and receives us.

Every single one.

12

A TALE OF TWO CHURCHES

In this and the following two chapters, we are going to talk about two churches. We could also subtitle it "The Rapture Church" or "The Church Left Behind." It is an account of two separate and distinct churches that were functioning at the same time but in very different ways.

Chapters 12 and 13 focus on two distinct people groups. We will be looking at two parts of the same church, one operating in gross darkness, while the other has the light of God all over them. There is not a separate age of darkness and light, and scripture says that, in fact, the group in the dark and the group in the light live life simultaneously. One group is raptured, while the other is left behind.

The following verse plainly describes the two distinct groups:

> Arise, shine; for thy light is come, and the glory
> of the Lord is risen upon thee.
>
> For, behold, the darkness shall cover the earth,
> and gross darkness the people: but the Lord shall

arise upon thee, and his glory shall be seen upon thee. (Isaiah 60:1–2)

In the book of Revelation, you can find these churches documented. In chapters 2 and 3, there are references to seven churches, in the following locations:

- Ephesus
- Smyrna
- Pergamos
- Thyatira
- Sardis
- Philadelphia
- Laodicea

These churches, no longer in existence, were all located in what would now be modern-day Turkey. However, many prophecy-intensive Bible scholars believe that not only were these real churches in real locations, but there were also specific messages to them.

We know that the book of Revelation is a prophetic book that tells of the activities related to the time just before and during the end of days and the Lord's coming for His church. The Lord's coming is a two-part situation. In the first part, Jesus comes back *for* the church. In His second appearing, seven years later, He comes back *with* the church.

From the list of the seven churches mentioned in the book of Revelation, I want to discuss the last two in more detail: the church in Philadelphia and the Laodicean Church. These were two churches in two separate and distinct geographical locations. Many end-time prophetic Bible scholars believe, however, that in addition to being in two different places, these churches were types, having characteristics of what would be found in the age to come. They were churches that we would see in operation as we come to the Lord's appearing or His coming for the saints. These two churches give us prophetic insight into what the conditions are when the Lord comes.

13

THE CHURCH IN PHILADELPHIA

We find the first church, the church in Philadelphia, mentioned in Revelation 3:7–12:

> And to the angel of the church in Philadelphia write; These things saith he that is holy, he that is true, he that hath the key of David, he that openeth, and no man shutteth; and shutteth, and no man openeth;
>
> I know thy works: behold, I have set before thee an open door, and no man can shut it: for thou hast a little strength, and hast kept my word, and hast not denied my name.
>
> Behold, I will make them of the synagogue of Satan, which say they are Jews, and are not, but do lie; behold, I will make them to come and worship before thy feet, and to know that I have loved thee.

Because thou hast kept the word of my patience, I also will keep thee from the hour of temptation, which shall come upon all the world, to try them that dwell upon the earth.

Behold, I come quickly: hold that fast which thou hast, that no man take thy crown.

Him that overcometh will I make a pillar in the temple of my God, and he shall go no more out: and I will write upon him the name of my God, and the name of the city of my God, which is new Jerusalem, which cometh down out of heaven from my God: and I will write upon him my new name.

In the other churches mentioned, the Lord rebukes or corrects things, saying, "You have a little strength, but I have somewhat against you." You find Him saying things like that to most of the churches, but not the Philadelphia Church; they are different. There is no rebuke. You won't hear the statement, "I have somewhat against thee." God said that He was pleased with this church, and He was satisfied with what they had done.

Philadelphia Means Love

The word *Philadelphia* comes from the Greek word *phileo* and carries with it the meaning of brotherly love. Two other Greek words that describe love are *agape* and *eros*. Agape is the love of God or godly love, and Eros is erotic love. The Philadelphia Church exhibited brotherly love.

- Philia: brotherly love
- Agape: the love of God
- Eros: erotic love

As you go through this scripture, you will find some things that pleased the Lord. He tells us in the latter part of verse 8 that He was delighted with the Philadelphia Church for two main reasons: They kept His Word and didn't deny His name. They were a church of the Word. They were not a church that went along with whatever the rest of society was doing. The church can't just make things up as they go along.

> I know thy works: behold, I have set before thee an open door, and no man can shut it: for thou hast a little strength, and hast **kept my word, and hast not denied my name**. (Revelation 3:8, emphasis added)

God is not about progressive revelation, other than we can know Him better the more we spend time with Him, and He may progressively reveal more of Himself to us over time. So what He said, He meant, and He does not change. He is not a God who is progressive on how He thinks about issues. When God tells us something in His Word, we should not only believe it; we should put it into practice.

You know as well as I do that in the process of learning anything—hitting a golf ball, riding a bicycle, playing a sport or a musical instrument, for example—there is a pretty good chance you will fall short of perfection from time to time. It is an absolute. The same thing applies to living by faith in God's Word. As we practice the truths of His Word and learn how to live the way He wants us to, we are sometimes going to fail.

We all do. None of us make it without falling and stumbling. We are not perfect.

However, God has given us a provision through Jesus Christ to help us with our failures. He said that if we confessed our sins, He would be faithful and just to forgive us. We know that in our imperfections, the Lord has given us grace—and lots of it. God does not demand perfection from us, but He does expect us to shoot for it.

Confession Is Not Enough

With that being said, should we continue to sin just because God will forgive us? Absolutely not. Here is what the book of Romans says about it:

> What shall we say then? Shall we continue in sin, that grace may abound?
>
> God forbid. How shall we, that are dead to sin, live any longer therein?
>
> Know ye not, that so many of us as were baptized into Jesus Christ were baptized into his death? (Romans 6:1–3)

God does not like that way of thinking very much; in fact, He forbids it. Someone might say, "Lord, I just can't help how I am; the temptations are just too strong. You know I'm just a sinner; so I'm justified when I mess up, right?"

That might sound good to you, but the Bible says you have to strive to do things the right way. However, Jesus said that when you fail, He would be there to catch you and forgive you, but you still have to try. We should put our best effort out there every time. We must grow and work at this thing.

According to Jesus, the church at Philadelphia was honorable, kept His Word, and refused to deny His name. That is significant because I believe many people are ashamed of the name of Jesus. In many instances, we have reduced His name down to just "Christ"—not Jesus Christ. Christ is not His name; it is the definition of who He is and what He does. Christ means anointed. Jesus is His name.

There is absolutely nothing wrong with using "Christ" when referencing Jesus. However, sometimes we tend to polish this thing up to the point that we no longer identify with the man named Jesus. We tend to identify more with some religious figure, some iconic structure of the faith—the Christ. Never forget, however, that it was not just Christ who hung on the cross; it was the man of flesh and bone, named Jesus.

The Great Commission: Are You Willing?

That same Jesus proclaimed that through faith in His name, people would be healed, delivered, and set free. Therefore, to keep the name of Jesus is to be willing to not only use it but also to do all the things done in His name.

We have been commissioned by God to go everywhere in the known world and preach the Good News of the Gospel to everyone. We should lay hands on the sick, and they will recover. We should expect to see miraculous signs as we use the name of Jesus. As we are obedient to do the things that Jesus told us to do, people will be set free. In contrast, if we are ashamed to do those things in His name, we have not kept the name.

Jesus spoke about that in Mark 16:15–17:

> And he said unto them, Go ye into all the world, and preach the gospel to every creature.
>
> He that believeth and is baptized shall be saved; but he that believeth not shall be damned.
>
> And these signs shall follow them that believe; In my name shall they cast out devils; they shall speak with new tongues.

And in the latter part of verse 18, he said:

> They shall lay hands on the sick, and they shall recover. (Mark 16:18)

A church that is unwilling to lay hands on the sick does not fit in that category. It is not following the full commission of what Jesus commanded them to do. For example, Jesus took the little children who were brought to Him, laid His hands on them, and blessed them. Even today, we follow His example and bless people in the name of Jesus. The church subscribes to the laying on of hands in Jesus's name for many reasons. Here are just a few.

- The apostle Paul said that we wage a good warfare with the prophecies that went before us through the laying on of hands.
- Sometimes we prophesy to people through the laying on of hands and in the name of Jesus.
- Impartation of the gifts of the Spirit can be accomplished by the laying on of hands.
- Devils and demons are cast out and placed under control by the laying on of hands in the name of Jesus.

He Is Talking about Power

Jesus was talking about the power available to us in His name. The church at Philadelphia was not ashamed of His Word or to use and exercise His name. They were supporters and defenders of the Word of God and were not willing to alter their beliefs with every wind of doctrine that blew through. They were courageous in the use of His name. Notice what it says about the Philadelphia Church in verse 10:

> Thou hast kept the word of my patience. (Revelation 3:10a)

It would also be correct to say, "You have kept My word with the power of endurance." They were not willing to give up using the name of Jesus every time somebody wanted to take it away from them. They had an enduring quality and an enduring power by God, and in Jesus's name, they stood against the works of the devil.

> Because thou hast kept the word of my patience,
> I also will keep thee from the hour of temptation,

which shall come upon all the world, to try them
that dwell upon the earth. (Revelation 3:10)

Remember, the Philadelphia Church is a prophetic church
that will be in place at the coming of the Lord. So if we are
the rapture generation, this church—this people group—is on
the earth today.

God told them that because they were not ashamed of Him—
because they had kept His Word and had patiently endured
trials and difficulties while standing steadfast in the face of
them—that He would save them from the hour of temptation
that is coming upon the world.

This hour of temptation, most Bible scholars would agree, is
the seven-year period that we refer to as the Tribulation, the
last three and a half years of the Great Tribulation. This hour
of temptation is coming upon the entire world, but the Bible
says the church in Philadelphia is protected from that time of
temptation.

Just Like the Ark

An excellent type and shadow of this would be the Ark. When
judgment fell on the earth in the form of a catastrophic flood,
God put eight people inside the Ark alongside the animals, and
they floated on top of the water—above the judgment. That
was a type of the rapture. We are also going to be above the
judgment that is coming upon the earth. We are not even going
to be here on the planet when all of it takes place; we will be in
heaven, far above it, when the hammer falls.

People Are Getting Saved

"Well, I see from the Bible that people are still getting saved during the Tribulation." Of course, you do. Remember, this is a time of Jacob's trouble. There are going to be 144,000 evangelists coming out of Israel to take the gospel to the world, but they will not be the only ones preaching it—not by a long shot. The Bible says that even the angels will be preaching the gospel during those days. They don't preach it now, but they will in that dispensation, and multitudes of people will come into the Kingdom of God because of them.

"But won't the saints go through the Tribulation?" you ask.

Yes, there will be some, but those who have kept the Word, have not denied the name of Jesus, and have been patiently enduring the forces of the day—which are going to increase the closer we get to the Tribulation—will be saved by God from the Tribulation. Remember: Jesus said in Revelation 3 that He is going to keep this group of people from the time of temptation and the great Tribulation that is going to come upon the earth:

> Because thou hast kept the word of my patience,
> I also will keep thee from the hour of temptation,
> which shall come upon all the world, to try them
> that dwell upon the earth. (Revelation 3:10)

There are twenty-one judgments—subdivided into three sets of seven—mentioned in Revelation 6–18. There are seven seal judgments, seven trumpet judgments, and seven vial judgments (sometimes translated as "bowl" judgments). The vials are poured out, the trumpet sounds, and the seals are opened.

After chapter 3, the word *church* (or any reference to it) is never mentioned again until chapter 22. The church is strangely absent while the judgment is happening. That is noteworthy because we are spared from the judgment and are living above it.

The Philadelphia Church Is the Rapture Church

> Husbands, love your wives, even as Christ also loved the church, and gave himself for it;
>
> That he might sanctify and cleanse it with the washing of water by the word,
>
> That he might present it to himself a glorious church, not having spot, or wrinkle, or any such thing; but that it should be holy and without blemish. (Ephesians 5:25–27)

It is very apparent in this verse that when Jesus comes, the church will be without spot or blemish. In another place, it says without spot, wrinkle, or blemish. He is coming for what we refer to as the Glorious Church. And here in the middle of all this, we have just what Isaiah said: the glory shall be upon one group and darkness upon another:

> Arise, shine; for thy light is come, and the glory of the Lord is risen upon thee.
>
> For, behold, the darkness shall cover the earth, and gross darkness the people: but the Lord shall arise upon thee, and his glory shall be seen upon thee. (Isaiah 60:1–2)

So the account of this church—the Philadelphia Church—is the glorious church that Jesus is returning to gather up. He is talking about us. We are spared from the judgment.

> For the Lord himself shall descend from heaven with a shout, with the voice of the archangel, and with the trump of God: and the dead in Christ shall rise first:
>
> Then we which are alive and remain shall be caught up together with them in the clouds, to meet the Lord in the air: and so shall we ever be with the Lord. (1 Thessalonians 4:16–17)

"Caught up" is the phrase where the word *rapture* originates. The catching up of the church. The Lord keeps us out of this hour of temptation by this thing called the rapture—the catching away. We will be caught up to meet the Lord in the air. And so shall we ever be with the Lord.

> Wherefore comfort one another with these words. (1 Thessalonians 4:18)

We should comfort one another with His words. He said those words should be encouraging to those who understand them.

I become grieved in my spirit when I see what is happening around us—grieved not for me, but for those who may not know the Lord. Without question, pandemonium is coming upon this planet, but the good news is that God said He is going to take us above and out of harm's way. I am ready to be caught up. Are you ready?

14

THE CHURCH AT LAODICEA

The second church that we are going to talk about is the Laodicean Church. And just like the church at Philadelphia, it is mentioned in Revelation 3:14–20:

> And unto the angel of the church of the Laodiceans write; These things saith the Amen, the faithful and true witness, the beginning of the creation of God;

> I know thy works, that thou art neither cold nor hot: I would thou wert cold or hot.

> So then because thou art lukewarm, and neither cold nor hot, I will spue thee out of my mouth.

> Because thou sayest, I am rich, and increased with goods, and have need of nothing; and knowest not that thou art wretched, and miserable, and poor, and blind, and naked:

> I counsel thee to buy of me gold tried in the fire, that thou mayest be rich; and white raiment,

that thou mayest be clothed, and that the shame of thy nakedness do not appear; and anoint thine eyes with eyesalve, that thou mayest see.

As many as I love, I rebuke and chasten: be zealous therefore, and repent.

Behold, I stand at the door, and knock: if any man hear my voice, and open the door, I will come in to him, and will sup with him, and he with me.

In verse 20, Jesus is knocking on the door of a church—His church—waiting for someone to let Him in. Originally, the church was formed and built upon His name, for the sole purpose of doing His work. They are supposed to be preaching His Word and ministering to the people, just like the Philadelphia Church, yet here He is, outside and knocking, trying to get in.

We use verse 20 a great deal to invite people to receive salvation. We use it many times metaphorically in examples such as, "Behold, He knocks at the door of your heart." I don't have a problem using it that way, but in the context of this verse, Jesus is trying to physically step inside a church that's supposed to represent Him, and He's not allowed entrance.

A Tepid Church

I want you to notice something else about this church. The Bible says that they are not cold or hot but are lukewarm. The word *lukewarm* means tepid or close to room temperature. If you put your hand in water that was close to your body temperature, you wouldn't feel it. You wouldn't even know you're getting wet. It would not have an effect on you.

What Jesus is saying is that the Laodicean Church was so tepid, its presence was never felt; it made no impression. They had no conviction, no power to change society or a person's life—a neutral organization that did nothing to change the hearts and lives of the people associated with it. It has no anointing, no conviction, and no power.

That's why Jesus said that it would be better for them—and He would also like it better—if they were either cold or hot. If they were one or the other, they would surely have a clue of their situation. If people get cold in their relationship with God, they know it. Conversely, if they were hot and on fire for God, they would know that too. Being lukewarm, or tepid, constitutes the absence of feeling anything. Nothing moves them.

Religion: The Opiate of the People

Karl Marx is not someone I valued highly. In fact, I don't agree with much of anything he had to say, with the possible exception of one thing: He said that religion was the opiate of the people. The reason I agree with that one thing is that Jesus said it long before Marx drew his first breath.

Marx's "opiate of the people" comment is exactly what Jesus is talking about here. Jesus told us that there was a neutralizing effect from going to church. He said that it would be easy for us to think that we're okay and everything is great with our spiritual lives, just because we are sitting in church every time the doors open. We assume everything is fine simply because we have been baptized, we show up for church services, and our name is in the membership database.

You are so tepid.

Just being baptized and joining the church will not do you any good, in and of itself. There is only one thing, one act of your will that is going to help you, and that is the act of being born again. As Jesus said to Nicodemus in John 3:1–7:

> There was a man of the Pharisees, named Nicodemus, a ruler of the Jews:
>
> The same came to Jesus by night, and said unto him, Rabbi, we know that thou art a teacher come from God: for no man can do these miracles that thou doest, except God be with him.
>
> Jesus answered and said unto him, Verily, verily, I say unto thee, Except a man be born again, he cannot see the kingdom of God.
>
> Nicodemus saith unto him, How can a man be born when he is old? can he enter the second time into his mother's womb, and be born?
>
> Jesus answered, Verily, verily, I say unto thee, Except a man be born of water and of the Spirit, he cannot enter into the kingdom of God.
>
> That which is born of the flesh is flesh; and that which is born of the Spirit is spirit.

Marvel not that I said unto thee, Ye must be born again.

If you have not been born again in the Spirit, and if your spirit has not been made new by the power of Almighty God, church membership at the end of your life will do nothing for you. It will do you no good at all. In fact, Jesus said:

> Jesus saith unto him, I am the way, the truth, and the life: **no man cometh unto the Father, but by me.** (John 14:6, emphasis added)

Jesus is the doorway that you must go through. Religion is not enough. Karl Marx was right in that religion is a drug that people take to satisfy something inside of them, but in the end, it means nothing. It looks good, feels good, and will make you think you are okay, but in reality, it will blind you. It will anesthetize you to the point that you won't be able to determine your own condition.

> I know thy works, that thou art neither cold nor hot: I would thou wert cold or hot. (Revelation 3:15)

Know Your Condition

Jesus wants you hot or cold. The Laodicean people were not aware of their spiritual temperature. They had no idea if they were hot or cold. They were lukewarm but couldn't even comprehend it. Do you know your spiritual temperature? The Laodicean people had no idea.

> Because thou sayest, I am rich, and increased
> with goods, and have need of nothing.
> (Revelation 3:17a)

The Laodiceans were not aware of their spiritual condition, much like you may not be fully aware of yours. You may find yourself saying similar things about yourself, as well: "I don't need anything. Everything is fine with me. I'm okay, and you're okay; we're all okay."

People console themselves in their unbelief. They congregate in large groups, where they can validate one another. You'll hear things like:

- "Come on, man; you're okay."
- "You don't need to bring that up; you don't need that."
- "Don't get too deep in that Bible. It will mess you up."
- "You don't want anything to do with that 'getting filled with the Holy Spirit' stuff. That's nothing but crazy talk."

People like that will validate your unbelief and condition. Because there's a smokescreen of deception in the crowd, they will tell you that you are okay when, in fact, you are far from it.

> Because thou sayest, I am rich, and increased
> with goods, and have need of nothing; and
> knowest not that thou art wretched, and
> miserable, and poor, and blind, and naked.
> (Revelation 3:17)

I'm not pointing my finger at anybody, but there are serious, sober-minded phrases used here. Let's take a closer look at a couple of them.

Blind and Naked

The scriptures say that there is a blindness associated with this. There is a religious and spiritual blindness in this group of people that prevents them from seeing the truth when it's right in front of them.

The scripture also says that they were naked as well as blind. Now, the reason the word *naked* is so important here is that you have to be clothed in a robe of righteousness before you can stand before the Lord. If you don't have the cloak of righteousness given to you by the precious blood of the Lamb, you are considered naked and not entitled to stand before Him.

Remember the guy in the Bible who came to the wedding of the king without proper clothes? It caused him quite a bit of embarrassment, to say the least:

> And when the king came in to see the guests, he saw there a man which had not on a wedding garment:
>
> And he saith unto him, Friend, how camest thou in hither not having a wedding garment? And he was speechless.
>
> Then said the king to the servants, Bind him hand and foot, and take him away, and cast him

into outer darkness, there shall be weeping and gnashing of teeth.

For many are called, but few are chosen. (Matthew 22:11–14)

Folks, you cannot go to a wedding without the proper clothes. Keep your camouflage hunting jacket in the closet and put on a suit. I am talking about the Marriage Supper of the Lamb, after all. It is the Wedding and a huge deal. You have to be suitably clothed. Jesus is making a spiritual reference here. He said there is a spiritual blindness that causes people to believe that they are clothed when they are not. That is what religion does to people.

What a Contrast

There is an enormous contrast between the two churches. On the one hand, there is the Philadelphia Church. God said that because they kept His Word and kept His name, all the while enduring difficulty, He is going to keep them from the hour of temptation. He is going to save them from the coming judgment. However, notice the entirely different fate the Laodiceans are facing:

So then because thou art lukewarm, and neither cold nor hot, I will spue thee out of my mouth. (Revelation 3:16)

It's important to note that one group—the Philadelphia Church—is kept from or kept above the judgment, while another—the Laodicean Church—is spewed out of God's mouth and finds itself going through the Tribulation without deliverance of any kind. One church is delivered, and the other is left behind. There is a whole group of church folk who are not going when the trumpet sounds. Did you know that? A sobering thought, isn't it? I cannot tell you precisely who is in that group, who doesn't make the trip, but I can tell you without a doubt who does get on that bus: Me. I have already made arrangements.

In the first part of Revelation 3:18, God said:

> I counsel thee to buy of me gold tried in the fire.

"Gold tried in the fire" is an interesting phrase. Look in 1 Peter1:7:

> That the trial of your faith, being much more precious than of gold that perisheth, though it be tried with fire, might be found unto praise and honour and glory at the appearing of Jesus Christ.

He is talking about a life of faith. This Laodicean Church had not put their faith in God. In fact, there was no faith in the house. You are born again by faith in God. That is the ticket to freedom.

You may say, "Well this must be a 'faith versus works' thing; it must be that one church is good, and the other church—not so much."

No, it's not that at all.

How Do We Qualify?

> For the Lord himself shall descend from heaven
> with a shout, with the voice of the archangel,
> and with the trump of God: and the dead in
> Christ shall rise first. (1 Thessalonians 4:17)

So to qualify to be in this first church, we have to be in Christ. Good works will not cause you to be worthy of the rapture. You have to be in Christ. You see, the Laodicean people were not in Christ and had no faith. But you can be in Christ. You can have faith. Be ready; Jesus is not going to leave His body behind.

God admonished them to be clothed in white raiment. We see in Revelation 19:7–8:

> Let us be glad and rejoice, and give honour to
> him: for the marriage of the Lamb is come, and
> his wife hath made herself ready.

> And to her was granted that she should be
> arrayed in fine linen, clean and white: for the
> fine linen is the righteousness of saints.

That garment mentioned here is the robe of righteousness we receive when we come to the Lord. We don't get it because of our good works of righteousness—all the fine things we have done—but by the blood of Jesus that redeemed us under God. Righteousness is not something we receive because we are good; it is just because we are in Him.

Nothing Is More Important

Do you understand how important these truths are in the day and hour in which we are living? They are critical. I feel a tremendous spiritual responsibility to the Body of Christ because I know what is going on. I didn't just learn this yesterday. I know it deep down in my spirit. There is an entire world out there that doesn't understand what I'm showing you. They don't understand that they must be born again. Church membership by itself will not help them.

Dr. Kenneth Hagin was a great evangelist and teacher. He often gave a detailed account of when he physically died and began to descend into hell. He did not merely dream of his death; He actually died. As he was on his way to hell, he knew what was happening. Three times he descended, and three times he was pulled back to life.

His spirit left his body, and he began his trip to hell. As he started his descent, he began yelling (he was in the Spirit, and people couldn't physically hear his screams), "I'm saved; I'm saved; I'm a member of the First Baptist Church." He was shouting because he knew where he was headed and could not do anything about it.

Church membership did not do Kenneth Hagin any favors. Being a member of a church will not save you, either, because it takes more than good works to make it to heaven. Good works alone will not save you. You have to be in Christ.

This Laodicean Church could actually be called an institutional church because it is in the business of religion. It has a business mind-set with a hierarchical structure, without Christ found in it anywhere. There will be many icons and statues, with many formulas and religious exercises that are used to promote their religious lifestyle. They may serve the Eucharist and the Lord's Supper, and then they may sign you up. They may also baptize you in water, but let me be clear, not one of those things will do you any good if you do not know Jesus Christ as your personal Savior. Not one. You must be born again.

Being Lukewarm Is No Joke

Jesus said this to the Laodicean Church:

> So then because thou art lukewarm, and neither cold nor hot, I will spue thee out of my mouth. (Revelation 3:16)

Some translations say that He would vomit them out of His mouth:

> So then, because you are lukewarm, and neither cold nor hot, I will vomit you out of My mouth. (Revelation 3:16 NKJV)

The Backslidden Church

Those folks left behind are in the backslidden church—the worldly church, the morally loose church. You could also say it's the "It Doesn't Matter How You Live or What You Do" church. They have traded a relationship with Jesus Christ for social acceptability, political correctness, tolerance of sin, and motivational teaching.

They are what we would refer to as a feel-good church. They have traded a true relationship with Jesus for being cool and a walk in the world. They have a tendency to be focused more on light shows and video presentations—anything considered cool and trendy—than a relationship with Jesus Christ. They want all the benefits of Christianity with none of the responsibilities. That is the institutional church.

There is a cathedral in Washington DC where Muslims and so-called Christians have merged into one church. I can tell you right now that that is not going to work. You cannot water down this gospel. Not all roads lead to the Lord. There are not ten or twenty ways to the Lord; there is one way and one way only. The Bible says:

> Jesus saith unto him, I am the way, the truth, and the life: no man cometh unto the Father, but by me. (John 14:6)

You can find this Laodicean Church outlined in another couple of places:

> Now we beseech you, brethren, by the coming of our Lord Jesus Christ, and by our gathering together unto him. (2 Thessalonians 2:1)

That verse is talking about Jesus's coming. That is the rapture of the church when we are gathered together to Him.

> That ye be not soon shaken in mind, or be troubled, neither by spirit, nor by word, nor by letter as from us, as that the day of Christ is at hand.

> Let no man deceive you by any means: for that
> day shall not come, except there come a falling
> away first, **and that man of sin be revealed**,
> the son of perdition. (2 Thessalonians 2:2–3,
> emphasis added)

"That man of sin" Paul is referring to in verse 3 is the antichrist, who will not be revealed until after the rapture of the church takes place. That is the first seal that is opened according to Revelation 6. The rider on the white horse is the antichrist. Here's what it says:

> And I saw when the Lamb opened one of the
> seals, and I heard, as it were the noise of thunder,
> one of the four beasts saying, Come and see.

> And I saw, and behold a white horse: and he
> that sat on him had a bow; and a crown was
> given unto him: and he went forth conquering,
> and to conquer. (Revelation 6:1–2)

Paul said that there would first be a falling away:

> Let no man deceive you by any means: for that
> day shall not come, **except there come a falling
> away first**, and that man of sin be revealed, the
> son of perdition. (2 Thessalonians 2:3, emphasis
> added)

The Supreme Court vote that legalized same-sex marriage and made it a recognized part of America's lifestyle is described right there in that verse. When the church cheers for that kind of ruling, and the professional clergy is willing to compromise at that level, that is unacceptable behavior. What are the followers of these church leaders doing if the leaders themselves are setting that kind of example?

The institutional church is not sufficient for you. A relationship with Jesus Christ is the important thing. Signing a membership card and becoming a member in good standing of some church is not the same thing as a relationship with Jesus Christ. The professionals are telling us how to have a relationship with the Lord when they have never had one themselves. Now we have the blind leading the blind, and they both are getting ready to fall into a ditch. It says so in Matthew 15:14:

> Let them alone: they be blind leaders of the blind. And if the blind lead the blind, both shall fall into the ditch.

I can tell you right now with certainty that I'm not going to fall in that ditch, and if you listen to me, neither will you. This is not an experiment; this is our eternal existence on the line.

The Laodicean Church is referenced again in 1 Timothy 4:1:

> Now the Spirit speaketh expressly, that in the latter times some shall depart from the faith, giving heed to seducing spirits, and doctrines of devils.

A person cannot depart from something they never had any more than they could leave Hawaii if they've never been there. They can't depart from the faith if they were never in faith to begin with.

> Speaking lies in hypocrisy; having their conscience seared with a hot iron. (1 Timothy 4:2)

With that in mind, do you think it matters what you give your attention to? Do you believe it's all okay? Do you say to yourself, "Well, God loves me. He's a good God, and He would never judge me"? You would be wise to examine those you allow to speak into your life.

15

THE RELIGION OF THE FALSE PROPHET

Universalism is the religion of the false prophet. You see that in Revelation 13. The false prophet demands that all people of all faiths worship the image of the beast—Christian, Muslim, and Buddhist, it doesn't matter. Universalism is the religion of the antichrist. However, the Lord said that there is only one way, not all ways.

"Well, a just God would not send anyone to hell," you may say.

I completely disagree. A just God would send us all to hell if we got what we deserved. However, Jesus intervened and gave us a reprieve.

Let's look at 1 Timothy 4:1–4:

> Now the Spirit speaketh expressly, that in the latter times some shall depart from the faith, giving heed to seducing spirits, and doctrines of devils;

Speaking lies in hypocrisy; having their conscience seared with a hot iron;

Forbidding to marry, and commanding to abstain from meats, which God hath created to be received with thanksgiving of them which believe and know the truth.

For every creature of God is good, and nothing to be refused, if it be received with thanksgiving:

For it is sanctified by the word of God and prayer.

In this verse, you find that some people are departing from the faith. Some are giving their ear to seducing spirits and devilish doctrines to the point that their consciences no longer function as God intended. Let's look at 2 Timothy 4:1–2:

I charge thee therefore before God, and the Lord Jesus Christ, who shall judge the quick and the dead at his appearing and his kingdom;

Preach the word; be instant in season, out of season; reprove, rebuke, exhort with all long suffering and doctrine.

"Preach the Word." That's what Paul told the man of God to do.

Paul said that even though he would not be present in the flesh, he entrusted us to God and His Word. It is vitally important that we become students of God's Word. He said it would build us up and give us an inheritance. He commended the

Ephesian believers to the Word. When your pastor isn't around any longer, the Word of God will build you up and give you an inheritance in Christ Jesus. That's just the way it shakes out.

Paul told the man of God to preach the Word. He said to be instant in season and out of season. He said to be ready not only when it's convenient, but when it's not. Reprove, rebuke, exhort with all long-suffering. Here is what 2 Timothy 4:3 says:

> For the time will come when they will not endure sound doctrine; but after their own lusts shall they heap to themselves teachers, having itching ears.

There is an entire group of people who will not take correction or a rebuke. Instead, they go in search of teachers who will tell them what they want to hear. When I mentioned motivational speaking earlier, that's what I meant. There is nothing wrong with motivational speaking, in and of itself, if you are willing to endure the rebuke when it comes.

We need encouragement, but if that is all we get, we are not getting enough of what we need. Sometimes, God's Word will correct us to change us. It will tell us when we are not living right, and then we must be inclined to change. I can hear the Lord say, "Perk it up, guys, and get with it." We must be willing and obedient.

But the scripture says that there was an entire group of people—the Laodicean Church—that would not allow that to happen. The Laodicean Church is the last-day church, the specific one we are talking about, so it has to be it. It was certainly not the Philadelphia Church, so it has to be the Laodiceans.

Remember what we just read in 2 Timothy above: "They heap to themselves teachers, having itching ears." These people are saying, "Tell me what I want to hear, or we're going to fire you and get someone else who will."

That is the institutional church. We have gimmicks and tricks, sideshows and slideshows, but people do not want to hear the truth of the Bible. That is the problem.

Universalism comes directly out of that. Tell me what I want to hear, and let me do what I want to do. It's hyper-grace. Don't misunderstand me: I'm all for the grace message, but hyper-grace allows you to live any way you please, without consequences, and that is just not okay.

Which Group Are You In?

We have looked in the Bible and discovered we are living in the time of the two churches. One church is red-hot and on fire for God. The other church is lukewarm and does not even know it; in fact, they have grown cold. God wants us to be in the "on fire and always ready" group.

> Watch ye therefore, and pray always, that ye may be accounted worthy to escape all these things that shall come to pass, and to stand before the Son of man. (Luke 21:36)

The essential point to all this is that some of us will be leaving, while others are going to be staying. The scripture is clear concerning each group. It is clear about the condition of the ones who are left behind. I wouldn't want to be in that crowd, would you?

1 Thessalonians 4:16 says,

> For the Lord himself shall descend from heaven with a shout, with the voice of the archangel, and with the trump of God: and the dead in Christ shall rise first:

If we are in Christ, then we are ready. But if we find ourselves walking at a distance from God, or if we are not walking with the Lord at all, we are definitely not ready. Make sure there isn't too much world hanging on you. Make sure you don't have too much attachment to this world. Get it straight.

God said to the Laodicean Church, "I exhort you to buy me gold tried in fire." He also said, "Behold, I stand at the door and knock."

The Laodicean Church was entrenched in the world, but Jesus said that if they would let Him in, He could fix it, right now, today. Let Him in.

16

THE GLORIOUS CHURCH

In Ephesians 5:25, Apostle Paul gives us insight into how we should view the marriage/church relationship:

> Husbands, love your wives, even as Christ also loved the church, and gave himself for it.

The biblical covenant of marriage is between one male husband and one female wife, regardless of what some high-court ruling may say to the contrary. Marriage should be patterned only after the relationship that Jesus had with the church. No other way. Many people think that the opposite is true, that the church should be patterned after the husband and wife. It's not so easy because of the way that marriage looks in our current social environment.

You must understand that the people behind the scenes—those people pulling strings on this issue—are after something more ominous than a man marrying another man, or a woman marrying another woman. They are after the freedom of the church. They want to seal your mouth closed and shut you down. That is their plan. You think it's one thing, but it is something else entirely. They are working from a different agenda altogether. The truth is that prophetically, the assault on marriage is an assault on the church.

The significant thing to remember is that the relationship between Christ and the church is what marriage is patterned after. It is the example of how Jesus loves His church. Jesus loves His church the way a husband is supposed to love his wife. Do you love your wife or husband? Certainly, you do. Following that logic, do you think Jesus cares about you? Do you think He cares about the condition of His church and the many assaults made against it? Without question, He does.

Do You Know Jesus or Know of Him?

Do you really know who Jesus is? He is not just a rabbi or a well-educated and gifted teacher. Neither is He merely a historical figure from the past. He is the Godhead of the church, creator of the universe, the Almighty God—who came to this earth in the form of a man. He is not just some random person.

Do you understand His capabilities? Do you realize how long it would take Him to put out their candle—take the Glory of God from them? How long is a heartbeat? It would be faster than that. Once you understand who He is, and who His opponents are, you will get a better sense of what is possible. I am forever and always on His side. No question, I am playing on His team.

Going back to Ephesians, Apostle Paul said there are three things in the church the Lord is not going to put up with: spots, wrinkles, and blemishes. Here is what Paul said:

That he might sanctify and cleanse it with the washing of water by the word,

That he might present it to himself a glorious church, not having spot, or wrinkle, or any such thing; but that it should be holy and without blemish. (Ephesians 5:26–27)

God Is Coming for a Glorious Church

God is coming for a glorious church. The root of the word *glorious* is *glory*, and it should be looked at as the magnificence of God manifested among us in many ways. That should not be a revelation to anybody.

Glorious is defined in Strong's Concordance (reference number 1741) as "splendid in glory, noble, gorgeous, and honorable." The Bible says that when Jesus comes, He is not coming for a weak, defeated, underground church; a church that is trying to make it and just barely getting by. Rather, He is coming for a splendid, glorious, and gorgeous church, a church that is manifesting His Shekinah glory, a church that manifests the acts of God.

When God's glory comes in the house, marvelous things begin to happen. It means that His glory, His power, and His divinity are revealed. Jesus is not coming for a church where there are no demonstrations of the Holy Spirit. There will be demonstrations of the Spirit and His power.

Manifestations of God's Glory

Manifestations of God's glory have been witnessed down through history. These demonstrations had a tremendous effect on both the surroundings and those who observed them.

For example, when Moses went up Mount Sinai to meet with God, the Shekinah glory manifested there. From their position at the base of the mountain, the people who were congregated there only saw what looked like encircling clouds and thunderstorms. They saw fire and lightning wrapped around it, but left unseen was Moses, standing in the presence of God. It wasn't a storm in the usual sense of the word but rather the manifested glory of God. The cloud around the mountain was for the protection of the people, as they could not safely look upon the glory; it was much too radiant and powerful.

As he made his way down the mountain, Moses had to wear a veil because the glory of God enveloped him. The Bible says that his face shone with the glory of God and was much too bright for anyone to look at straight on.

That is what we mean when we talk about the glory being manifested in the church. We are not talking about having a typical church service. We are not talking about a dead, cold, and dry religious experience; we are talking about the light, the fire, and the glory of God. Fire represents God's glory. When God said He would baptize you with the Holy Ghost and with fire, He was talking about the fire of His glory, not a literal fire in the woodstove.

When we are baptized in the Holy Spirit, marvelous things begin to happen. There are manifestations like the gifts of the

Spirit and other things that occur as a result. There is a fire that comes into us. So following the logic, if you lose your fire, it is because you are losing the glory. In one translation, God said that He not only wanted you filled with the Spirit, but He also wanted you aglow and burning with it. Let's look in the book of Romans, from the Classic Edition of the Amplified Translation:

> Never lag in zeal and in earnest endeavor;
> be aglow and burning with the Spirit, serving
> the Lord. (Romans 12:11 AMPC)

Repeatedly, the fire of God—that radiant glory of God—was manifested in, and on, His people. Just like Moses when he came down the mountain, his face shone with the glory of God. When Jesus stepped into God's glory on the Mount of Transfiguration, He was a manifestation of God's glory. He glowed. He became a brilliant light source wrapped in a powerful energy field.

The Shroud of Turin

I highly recommend that you do some research on the Shroud of Turin. I have studied it quite a bit, and from the extensive amount of time that I have invested in it, I am convinced of its authenticity. I do not see any other way that it could have happened.

The shroud is amazing. It has the same characteristics of a negative film image. When you look at it, and you reverse the image, it would be like looking at the negative of an old piece of film. You can see the figure. However, experts will tell you that the only way the transfer of the image could have taken place was by heat. It had to be burned into the shroud, not painted on it. The person wrapped in the shroud had to have generated such intense heat that it burned their image into it.

The Bible says that the Spirit of God and the glory of God raised Jesus from the dead. In light of that, I believe the image that transferred onto the shroud was caused by the glory of God radiating out from the inside of Jesus. That same glory was radiating from Moses after he was in the presence of God on the mountain.

Now, when the Bible says Jesus is coming for a glorious church, I think we ought to expect manifestations of His glory in the house. It should not be something spooky or unnerving, but it should be something we anticipate, as we walk in the presence of God.

Let's look at 1 Thessalonians 5:1–2:

> But of the times and the seasons, brethren, ye have no need that I write unto you.
>
> For yourselves know perfectly that the day of the Lord so cometh as a thief in the night.

"The day of the Lord" is talking about the thief coming in the night. On the other hand, when Jesus comes back and steps foot on the Mount of Olives, every eye shall see Him, and every eye shall behold Him. That is not how a thief in the night would work, would he? He certainly would not want a bunch of people standing around, watching him work. That is referencing the time when Jesus comes back *with* the church. The "coming as a thief" statement describes when He comes *for* the church.

When the Bible says, "For when they shall say, peace and safety," that's talking about the world that does not have the discernment that you have, people who think this stuff is silly. Let's look at it:

> For when they shall say, Peace and safety; then sudden destruction cometh upon them, as travail upon a woman with child; and they shall not escape.

> But ye, brethren, are not in darkness, that that day should overtake you as a thief. (1 Thessalonians 5:3–4)

That verse did not say that destruction would come upon you; it said it would come upon them, the unbelievers. Notice that He contrasted you with them. That is why we are talking about these things. You should be aware of these situations so they won't sneak up on you.

A Church Full of Light

One characteristic of the latter-day church is that it is not a church full of darkness but is a church full of light. It is to be full of life, light, and the glory of God's presence.

> But ye, brethren, are not in darkness, that that day should overtake you as a thief. (1 Thessalonians 5:4)

You are not in darkness. You are the children of light. Remember that when we talk about light, it can be referencing the light of God's glory as well. We are the children of the glory of God and of light.

17

WHAT IS LIFE?

There are answers to specific questions that continually elude scientists, no matter how far they dig, how far back they go, or how close they get to the core of things. No matter how hard they try, they never find them. There is one little question that puzzles them more than most. The question: What is life? What makes life, life?

I read an article some time back that said that science had already proclaimed that we had virtually reached immortality. Medical science, as well as the people who research this thing called life, have gone back as far as they can to try and find the origin of it. They ask questions among themselves and others, like:

- Where did life come from?
- What was the basis of life's origination?

After much debate, they deduced that the most straightforward definition of life is light—and when you talk about light, you are talking about life. Everything that emanates from that light is living. Life originates from light. Light exudes life. Jesus said that He was the light of the world.

In the beginning, God said, "Let there be light." Because of those four words, all life began to flow from it. The origin of life is light.

So when God talks about light, He's not talking about compact fluorescents or LED bulbs that we use to shave and read by, but about something altogether different: the origin of all life. When He speaks of the light of God, He's talking about you. He came to put His light in you and His glory on you.

What Is Man?

In Psalm 8, when the angels looked at man, they posed a question to God:

> What is man, that thou art mindful of him?
> and the son of man, that thou visitest him?
> (Psalm 8:4)

You must remember something about these angels. They had seen creation. They had seen God create. God created man on the sixth day. But before God created man, He had already created the fish, the birds, the elephants, the giraffes, the lions, and the tigers, as well as many other things. However, when He came to the formation of man, it took on a different type of creation altogether.

The angels, who had seen all this creation happen before their eyes, said,

> **What is man**, that thou art mindful of him?
> and **the son of man,** that thou visitest him?

> For thou hast made him a little lower than the
> angels, and hast crowned him with glory and
> honour. (Psalm 8:4–5, emphasis added)

The actual translation of verse 5 says, "For thou hast made him
a little lower than God, and hast crowned him with glory and
honour." Before man fell, he had the glory of God on him.

Naked and Not Ashamed

> And they were both naked, the man and his
> wife, and were not ashamed. (Genesis 2:25)

When you read that Adam and Eve were naked and not
ashamed, you might think that they were just running around
the Garden of Eden all naked and not a bit embarrassed about
it. However, that is not what was going on at all. The reason
they were not ashamed was that they were covered in the glory
of God and did not need clothing, the way we understand the
word. The light of God surrounded them.

However, when man fell into sin, he gave his God-given glory
to the devil, and Satan became the god of this world through
that step-down. Remember, man was created initially a little
lower than God and had the glory on him, but when he fell, he
fell lower than the angels. The glory that was on both Adam
and Eve disappeared, and they realized that they were both
naked.

> And when the woman saw that the tree was
> good for food, and that it was pleasant to the
> eyes, and a tree to be desired to make one wise,

she took of the fruit thereof, and did eat, and
gave also unto her husband with her; and he
did eat.

And the eyes of them both were opened, and
they knew that they were naked; and they sewed
fig leaves together, and made themselves aprons.
(Genesis 3:6–7)

But there is good news: When you leave this earth, you will
trade your earthly body in for a magnificent, glorified body. We
get our glory back.

The Glorified Body

After Jesus was raised from the dead, people saw Him for
all of forty days. He walked among His friends and others,
talking to them on the road—appearing, disappearing, then
appearing, and disappearing again. Folks would see Him down
by the lake, look away, and then He was gone. Jesus would walk
through walls and closed doors, as if they were not even there.
He could do that because His glorified body wasn't bound by
earthly constraints. Jesus had a glorified body, and the Bible
says that as He is, so are you. So what He has, you get.

We're talking about the glory of God manifesting on people.
When the glory of God manifests, sickness cannot stay. When
the glory of God manifests, lives change for the better.

Religion? Enough Already

Enough of religion. We don't need religion alone; we need Jesus.

We desperately need more than mere religion can give us. We need the power of Jesus Christ. We have to be born again from above. The same power that raised Jesus from the dead raised you from the dead too. The glory of God that came upon Jesus, and raised Him from the dead, is the same glory that came upon you when you were born again. Let's look at a couple of versions of Romans 8:11:

> But if the Spirit of him that raised up Jesus from the dead dwell in you, he that raised up Christ from the dead shall also quicken your mortal bodies by his Spirit that dwelleth in you. (KJV)

Here's how the Living Bible says it:

> And if the Spirit of God, who raised up Jesus from the dead, lives in you, he will make your dying bodies live again after you die, by means of this same Holy Spirit living within you.

The glory of God that came on Jesus—that raised Him from the dead—is the same glory that came on you when you were born again. Further, I believe that if you didn't have a life-changing experience, you didn't get the real thing. If you think that being born again is merely signing up on the church attendance sheet or just "getting religion," you have a surprise waiting for you, and it's not a good one.

By being born again, you received a new nature. You were born from above. You are no longer just the old man who underwent an overhaul. You are a new creature in Christ Jesus, filled with the glory and the life of Almighty God. That is what the glory of God means. It is not just some religious experience. The glory of the Most High God came on you in abundance.

> Ye are all the children of light, and the children of the day: we are not of the night, nor of darkness.
>
> Therefore let us not sleep, as do others; but let us watch and be sober. (1 Thessalonians 5:5–6)

The Glorious Church Is the Right Choice

The characteristic of this glorious church is that they are full of the life and the light of God. They are not in darkness, and they are not sleeping. They have godly characteristics: they are awake; they have a breastplate of faith; they walk in love and have a hope of salvation.

> But let us, who are of the day, be sober, putting on the breastplate of faith and love; and for an helmet, the hope of salvation. (1 Thessalonians 5:8)

1 Corinthians 1:10 sums everything up quite well:

> Now I beseech you, brethren, by the name of our Lord Jesus Christ, that ye all speak the same thing, and that there be no divisions among you; but that ye be perfectly joined together in the same mind and in the same judgment.

18

THE GLORY WILL NOT COME

One of the characteristics of the latter-day church is that the people are in one accord, in one faith, and in one heart. You can't get God's glory to manifest on a group of people who are always divided, bellyaching, complaining, and whining about everything imaginable. Humans are by nature selfish, and sinful humans are even more so.

Division of the people is one of the negative characteristics found in some churches that cause the glory of God to leave. We spent a good deal of time talking about the seven churches in the book of Revelation, and those that exhibited those qualities. We then focused on two of the seven churches, the Philadelphia Church and the Laodicean Church, which were very dissimilar in the way they went about God's business.

Don't Make Me Take Your Candle

The common denominator to all those churches was that Jesus Christ, the head of the church, was coming to visit all of them.

He said that if they did not obey Him, He would take their candle from its place.

The candle represented the glory of God that manifested on those churches. Subsequently, a church that had lost its candle meant it had lost its glory. The glory of God was no longer present. That was the candle of revelation. In some cases, where it referred to the candlestick, it was talking about the messenger to the church or an angelic visitation—the messenger who comes to the church with a revelation from heaven.

The Angel Whispered in My Ear

I have been visited by angels on at least a hundred separate occasions while I've been preaching in church. Some of you might look at me a little cross-eyed at that statement, thinking that I'm exaggerating, but I'm not. It's actually a conservative estimate—absolutely no embellishment. Various well-respected people in my congregation have told me that while I was preaching, they saw an angel standing beside me in the pulpit whispering in my ear. These events happened at random times, and the people who told me were sitting in different parts of the sanctuary from one another, having no idea what the other had said. They heard distinctly in the Spirit what the angel said, and they told me that I repeated to the congregation precisely what they had heard the angel say to me. I've been told that same thing over and over again—over a hundred times—to the point that I have no other choice but to believe it. That is the messenger to the church.

Don't Lose Your Candle

If the candle of the church has been removed, the messenger has been taken out of the way, as well. That is why you have sermons that are as dry as dust. There is no longer a message from heaven in the house. The glory is what brings the anointed message. If there is no glory, there is no anointing on the message. When the glory leaves, the anointing goes, as well. That is the meaning of the word *ichabod*, "The glory has departed."

When the Spirit Departs

What is sobering is that I have seen the Spirit of God depart from a particular church, but I have never seen Him return. I have watched that church as it continued going through religious motions, living off memories but without the anointing. I am in no way implying that the Holy Spirit was not ever present in that church; we know that He never leaves us or forsakes us. He is omnipresent. So when I say depart, I am talking about the absence of the manifestations of the Spirit.

People can do things to offend God. When that happens, He calls them out on it. He corrects them. He scolded five of those seven churches that we looked at in the book of Revelation and told them straight up that they did things that displeased Him. Among other things, He told them that they left their first love. When they did those things, He was telling them, "When I come to you with that kind of judgment, you had better do the right thing, or you will lose your place." That's why, as a part of the glorious church, we have to be very sensitive to what God wants. It's no longer just about our agenda. It's much bigger than that.

That is why division in the church is so damaging. It's because it is driven entirely by an individual's self-will. It does not consider at all what God may want. It is only concerned with selfish motives: "Well, I want it this way. I want it that way." It does not matter what you want. You are not the head of the church.

Quit Griping

People get in strife and fight over anything and everything you could imagine—the color of the carpet, the car the pastor drives, or even the location of a television camera. "Well, bless God, I don't like where they put that camera."

Well, don't look at it. Some people don't seem to care at all about what's important to the ministry and who may get helped because those cameras exist.

"That camera is in my way. I have to look around that thing."

Here's an idea: Move, and get another seat.

When people start griping all the time, they get a nasty spirit on them; they "get a gripe on them," as we say in the South. Eventually, nothing can please them. That spirit is deadly and is designed to steal the glory from the house. Remember, Jesus is coming for a church without spot, wrinkle, or blemish.

The best commentary on the Bible is the Bible itself. It says that out of the mouths of two or three witnesses, let every word be established. So if you want to know what something is, let the Bible tell you. It will define itself for you, if you let it.

> But chiefly them that walk after the flesh in the
> lust of uncleanness, and despise government. (2
> Peter 2:10a)

Those people do not like any government oversight or authority of any kind. You can almost hear the alarm bells clanging. Let's read on:

> Presumptuous are they, selfwilled, they are not
> afraid to speak evil of dignities. (2 Peter 2:10b)

Are you talking about things that you shouldn't? If you are, you could be a catalyst for creating strife in the church. You really must be careful because if there's more than one person in your church, there's always the potential for discord. The only reason you don't have strife in the church is that people have matured in God to the point where they recognize how dastardly it can be and refuse to allow it to manifest.

Anywhere people exist, the possibility of strife also exists. The devil knows how to push your buttons; you must be smart enough not to fall into his trap.

> Whereas angels, which are greater in power and
> might, bring not railing accusation against them
> before the Lord. (2 Peter 2:11)

The angels, who have more power than we do, would never gripe against authority:

> But these, as natural brute beasts, made to be
> taken and destroyed, speak evil of the things

that they understand not; and shall utterly perish in their own corruption;

And shall receive the reward of unrighteousness, as they that count it pleasure to **riot in the day time**. Spots they are and blemishes, sporting themselves with their own deceivings while they feast with you. (2 Peter 2:12–13, emphasis added)

What Are Spots?

Those who are considered spots are people who are, among other things, unafraid to speak about things they shouldn't and dislike an authority structure of any type. They are the spots that Jesus was talking about when He said that He is coming for a church without spot, wrinkle, or blemish. In a glorious church, you cannot remain in the glory of God if you are a spot because He is coming for a church without them.

The Bible calls these people who cause division and trouble in the church spots and blemishes: "Sporting themselves with their own deceivings while they feast with you." In other words, they come and sit down with you, trying to make you believe that they are good men, acting like they are one of you, while the whole time they are actually divisive as they can be.

They either don't have any life of God in them, or they have pushed it so far back under the bushel that the glory of God has taken a back seat to their desire of getting their way. Getting their way and making their point is more important than anything else in their lives. Proving their position and arguing their case is more important than the glory of God. Even if you are right, there are times when you need to close your mouth and shut up. The Bible says that whatsoever things are good, honest, just, and of a good report should be proclaimed, not just those things that make you look good.

You Can Be Right and Be Wrong

Paul said that the people were not ready to hear what he had to share with them, and he was right. It would have been misguided to share something that the people could not yet receive. There are times to speak up and make a point, but there are also times to keep quiet. So if you're dealing with people who can't receive what you have to say, the best thing to do is sit on that once-in-a-lifetime idea until you can get it done harmoniously. To bully your way over and through the will of the people will not endear you or your cause to anyone. Even if you're right, you'll still be wrong. The outcome won't be beneficial to you.

The Bible says to share ideas with others in a way that can be easily received. People will have a hard time accepting your plan if you share it in a manner that's not easily digestible.

> But the wisdom that is from above is first pure, then peaceable, gentle, **easy to be entreated**, full of mercy and good fruits, without variance, without hypocrisy. (James 3:17 ASV, emphasis added)

You may even have to modify your attitude somewhat. There is no room to feel righteously indignant because of an attitude problem: "Well, I know I'm right. I know the scripture." Maybe so, but you also need to take the time to get to know people a little bit, as well. Dole that stuff out in bite-size portions. You don't want to choke people.

You wouldn't pour twenty pounds of dog food into your little ten-pound dog's bowl at one time, would you? Of course not. You would carefully measure it out and give them the amount that's appropriate for their size. Any more than that would be irresponsible.

That is precisely the same way to deal with scripture. Give people only what they can embrace. Speak to people on their level. Making a point just to make a point can be divisive.

Continuing in the first part of 2 Peter 2:14:

> Having eyes full of adultery, and that cannot cease from sin; beguiling unstable souls.

Spots are people who cause division in the church.

There are two ways to think about the church. One way would be to think about it as the church universal—the worldwide church. It could be the church in Africa, Central or South America, North America, or the Church of Rome.

However, when God talks to you about the church, He is talking about the one you attend on a weekly basis—the one that requires you to accept responsibility for the way you treat the people who sit beside you, week in and week out. After all, it isn't difficult to be nice to people you don't know well. You might think you have a greater mission and a higher calling, but you don't. Just work on your neighbor right there beside you; that will be good enough.

19

THE ROCK POLISHER

Sister Sandpaper

It's easy to be friendly and gracious to people who are complete strangers or to those you have a limited history with. It's a bit tougher when the person who rubs you the wrong way is sitting beside you, someone you've known for twenty years.

Sister Sandpaper is someone God put in your life to help polish off your rough edges. Without a doubt you need some polishing, and Sister Sandpaper was designed perfectly for that job. She's like a rock polisher.

What's a Rock Polisher?

A rock polisher is a very simple device that utilizes a revolving canister—think of a clothes dryer on a much smaller scale—driven by a small electric motor. You place rocks inside the container, turn it on, and they tumble all over each other—just like your towels and socks. Surprisingly, many of them are made of plastic.

So how in the world are you going to wear down a rock with a piece of plastic? It's because the container itself doesn't polish them; they polish themselves by repeatedly colliding with one another. The more those rocks tumble and roll over each other, the smoother and shinier they become.

Go up into the mountains and pick out a good-sized rock from the side of a hill. It probably has an interesting shape and may have many rough and jagged edges protruding from it. It may be somewhat attractive with moss and several types of minerals like quartz on its surface, but it's still just an ordinary rock.

On the other hand, if you pick out a similar sized rock that has made its home in a quickly moving stream, it will be as smooth as glass, with no rough edges at all. Why? There are minerals in the water—where I live, it is mostly limestone—that wash over those rocks all day, every day. Over time, the movement of the water—containing those tiny little minerals—acts like sandpaper and wears off all the rough edges until you end up with a perfectly smooth river rock. It turns something once ugly, jagged, and ordinary into a beautiful, slick, shiny stone. There's a big difference.

It's What You're Exposed To

The rock's shape is determined by what it is exposed to. Rock polishes rock. Also, the Bible says, clearly talking about us, that iron sharpens iron:

> Iron sharpeneth iron; so a man sharpeneth the countenance of his friend. (Proverbs 27:17)

If you're going to grow into what you're supposed to become, you're going to have to be exposed to things that whittle away at you and file down your rough edges. The old you that's nothing but a jagged rock found on a hillside has to be polished to become a smooth river stone.

"Well, I don't want to be whittled and filed on."

No surprise there. I don't, either. However, that's what Mr. Bad Temper who sits beside you exposes in you. Your relationship with him reveals your temper. As uncomfortable as it may be, it has to happen for quality change to take place.

"But that person is mean and nasty and said some things to me that were downright cruel."

You're probably telling the absolute truth, but the important thing to remember is not what they said to you but how you responded to what they said.

"Pastor, how in the world do I process that?" you ask. "I'll tell you how I'm going to process it," you say. "I'm going to get on my cell phone, Facebook, Twitter, and every other social media outlet I can think of, and I'm going to run them down to everybody."

I'll Fix Them

You failed that test already. We want to fix other people by changing everything about them. The problem is, you can't. Do you even know what the word *fixing* means? In the South, we pronounce it "fixin'." It is a Southern pronunciation that could mean "getting ready to do something," or "I'm going to show them." "I'm fixin' to go." "I'm fixin' to show them."

If you feel like you have to fix someone, then fix them by the power of the Holy Spirit. The inside-out fixing, or change, is what lasts. It is not the outside-in kind. People only change from a changed heart. As the saying goes, "People convinced against their will are of the same opinion still." Preaching alone will not fix them.

Preaching, while it can help by exposing some cracks or shedding some light on specific issues, cannot fix anyone who refuses to change. The only people who are fixable are those who want to be. You cannot change someone just because you want them to change. It doesn't work that way. If they don't want it, you're wasting your time. Change is not going to occur until those individuals want it to happen.

There are going to be some spots among us, but a divided church full of them is not the spot-free church that God is coming for. If you have divisions in the church, you cannot have a glorious church. The glory of God will leave.

I've seen that Ichabod thing come on multiple churches, and I could see and feel the Spirit of God leave because of decisions they made. You could physically feel it leave the house. The members kept on attending and tried to have revival, but they were kidding themselves. The best thing you can do is to figure out what happened and move on. Get into a place where there is life. Don't hang around in a dead church, or you'll inherit that same spirit and become just like it. You have to be very careful using the word *ichabod* in relationship to a church because it truly is a cursed thing.

The glorious church is going to be the church without spot. Look at Acts 2:1–2:

> And when the day of Pentecost was fully come, they were all with one accord in one place
>
> And suddenly there came a sound from heaven as of a rushing mighty wind, and it filled all the house where they were sitting.

When the Holy Spirit came, He looked for people who were in one accord. He looked for harmony so the glory would manifest. Why do you think the disciples were in the upper room for so long? There were a lot of issues surrounding the situation of the cross. Peter had denied the Lord, and every one of the disciples except for John had forsaken Him. Every single one of them was hiding out.

Don't try to tell me that there wasn't a lot of working through things going on in that upper room. They were up there studying the Word together to figure out what the problems were. There was probably a lot of repenting going on, as well. I'm sorry, you're sorry, we're all sorry. That was exactly what was going on.

Suddenly, everyone in the room got in agreement. It had to be sudden because you couldn't keep all those people that way for very long. The truth is, if the church ever does get in one accord, Jesus better come quickly, because it won't last long.

> And they, continuing daily with one accord in the temple, and breaking bread from house to house, did eat their meat with gladness and singleness of heart,

> Praising God, and having favour with all the
> people. And the Lord added to the church daily
> such as should be saved. (Acts 2:46–47)

Notice what happened when everybody came together in one
accord: People got saved. The church grew when the people had
a harmony of heart and were in unity.

It is not hard to see what the devil wants to do to the church
body. He wants people at each other's throats for absurd and
senseless reasons. Satan wants us in strife over the color of the
carpet, arguing over methods of outreach, or debating which
missionaries to support. You find the first point of division in
Acts 6:1:

> And in those days, when the number of
> the disciples was multiplied, there arose
> a murmuring of the Grecians against the
> Hebrews, because their widows were neglected
> in the daily ministration.

There were people upset because the widows were being
neglected in the daily ministration (the distribution of food).
That, among other things, is why the office of the deacon was
established. The deacon was there to help with those issues so
that the apostles could give themselves to the word of God and
prayer. The division in the church was pulling the men of God
out of their place of prayer and ministering the Word, to deal
with the division in the house of God.

> And the multitude of them that believed were
> of one heart and of one soul: neither said any
> of them that ought of the things which he

> possessed was his own; but they had all things common.
>
> And with great power gave the apostles witness of the resurrection of the Lord Jesus: and great grace was upon them all. (Acts 4:32–33)

The great favor of God was on the people who possessed a harmony of heart and who saw love as the primary thing rather than getting their own way. In fact, getting their way was far, far less important than the mission, the goal, the task, and the primary issues.

> And by the hands of the apostles were many signs and wonders wrought among the people; (and they were all with one accord in Solomon's porch.
>
> And of the rest durst no man join himself to them: but the people magnified them.
>
> And believers were the more added to the Lord, multitudes both of men and women.) (Acts 5:12–14)

You see the power that unity commands in the church? Unity is the atmosphere in which the glory of God manifests. That is the most important thing that any church can have—much more than perfect doctrine. Your doctrinal belief system is critical, and what you teach is vitally important, but none of us knows everything.

More than anything else, God wants a church whose members walk in love and harmony with one another. That is what keeps division at bay. The church understands the seriousness of it and prepares a house where His glory can manifest. He is not after a faultfinding, finger-pointing, high-and-mighty group. He is after a loving group. The glory of God manifests in a house that is full of His love.

20

Same-Sex Marriage and the Rapture of the Church

Author's Note

As we continue, I think that it is important to point out that I wrote this chapter before the Supreme Court's ruling regarding same-sex marriage. The topic of same-sex marriage was an integral part of this book from the start, but because of the High Court's decision, I am going to deal with it a little differently and show how this decision fits in the prophetic plan of scripture. However, before that happens, it's important for you to understand what prophecy is and how it works.

There is an interesting observation in scripture where God tells us that He created the end from the beginning. That is an amazing thing. You need to understand that God is not limited by time. The things that constrain and contain us have no effect on Him. He knows the future before the future happens.

When God gives us insight into a prophetic event, He is not showing us what is destined to occur just because He wants it to happen. Rather, God, in our unfolding history, knows the propensity of our actions and the things we do in every circumstance. Since He knows our actions, He tells us beforehand what we will do—not that He chose it or ordained it.

"Since it has been prophesied, it must be God's will," people say. In a sense, it is prophetic because God is telling us what is coming, but it is not prophetic because He wants it to happen; it is prophetic because He understands the circumstances and the people involved. Again, He tells us what is going to happen before it happens. That is important, because in many people's minds, when they hear a prophetic truth, there is a belief that nothing can alter the outcome. As a result, they offer no resistance, and the prophetic word is automatically considered their destiny. That is not true, at all. Nonetheless, we see what we see, and we know what we know, so I want to show how things fit in a prophetic order. I want to bring you encouragement in the process.

I want to state clearly from the beginning that we love homosexual people, even though we do not embrace or condone their lifestyle. Although we do not agree with their behavior, we love them and are not here to intentionally hurt or harm anyone. We are here only to bring truth and revelation of God's Word to all who read this book. It is a message to bring God's truth and order into a chaotic world.

In this chapter, we are going to discuss same-sex marriage and how that dovetails prophetically into why I believe that we are the rapture generation. With that in mind, let's look at Genesis 2:21:

> And the Lord God caused a deep sleep to fall upon Adam, and he slept: and he took one of his ribs, and closed up the flesh instead thereof.

In verse 21, the word *rib* may or may not be a rib as we know it. It might, but if God took one, He put another back in its place. More importantly, God was dealing with cells and DNA—He took DNA from Adam and made a woman. Remember, God inspired this before people knew what DNA was. God is always ahead of the curve.

> And the rib, which the Lord God had taken from man, made he a woman, and brought her unto the man.
>
> And Adam said, This is now bone of my bones, and flesh of my flesh: she shall be called Woman, because she was taken out of Man.
>
> Therefore shall a man leave his father and his mother, and shall cleave unto his wife: and they shall be one flesh.
>
> And they were both naked, the man and his wife, and were not ashamed. (Genesis 2:22–25)

Adam and Eve were naked in the sense that they were not dressed in the usual way we now wear our clothing. They were clothed in the glory of God and were neither embarrassed nor ashamed. Before sin entered, clothing carried a different connotation.

God Initiated Marriage

God created the institution of marriage. Because of that, we mortals cannot define marriage because we did not originate it. It makes no difference what we say about it or how we explain it, because the only one who can describe what marriage is, or what it is not, is God. He created it, so He alone can define it. His definition is the only one that matters.

God's very first covenant—long before His covenants with Abraham, Noah, or Job—concerned marriage. Before any of the major covenants took place with any of those men, the marriage covenant came first. (Note: I will not present an exhaustive study on them now, but it would be an excellent Bible study for you to undertake. Search for the word *covenant*, sharpen your pencil, and dive on in.)

Malachi 2:14 (emphasis added) bears this out:

> Yet ye say, Wherefore? Because the Lord hath been witness between thee and the wife of thy youth, against whom thou hast dealt treacherously: yet is she thy companion, and the **wife of thy covenant**.

Marriage was so important to God that He made a marital covenant. That is why it is out of order for people to live together out of wedlock. There is absolutely no biblical context for sex in any form apart from marriage. Premarital sex, as well as adulterous sex with anyone other than your husband or wife, is always forbidden. In that same vein, scripture also forbids same-sex relationships. In fact, according to the Word of God, the only context for sex is within the confines of marriage, period, end of story. There is no other way that God condones sex.

I was reading some information about the decade of the 1930s, concerning Adolf Hitler and his war machine. Hitler was just coming into power, and the world had not yet seen the impact that he would eventually bring to bear. In those years, Joseph Goebbels was his minister of propaganda. Goebbels said that if you tell a lie long enough, people will get to the point where they believe it as if it were true. The idea is to say something over and over again until people embrace it as truth.

The most effective way to replace the truth is to repeatedly reinforce the lie until it is accepted as the truth and the truth is acknowledged as the lie. Scripture says that there is a day coming when people will believe lies as being truth and will be damned:

> And for this cause God shall send them strong delusion, that they should believe a lie:
>
> That they all might be damned who believed not the truth, but had pleasure in unrighteousness. (2 Thessalonians 2:11–12)

It does not matter whether you believe the truth or not; it cannot be altered in any way. God is not going to do a rewrite just because society has changed and wanted Him to insert an addendum or two. Forget about it. You do not get a revision of God's Word, even though you think your case is a one-in-a-million kind of special. God is not going to give you a new version of the Bible to fit your particular indulgences. You may want Him to change things, but it is not going to happen. You have to adapt to God—He is not going to change just for your perceived benefit.

One Man and One Woman

In over six thousand years of recorded human history, the union between one man and one woman is the only way marriage has ever been recognized. There have been some deviations, but they have always ended in disaster. For over two thousand years of church history, marriage has been between a man and a woman—male and female.

The tradition of marriage—a tradition that has been ingrained in society and understood by Christians and non-Christians, believers and nonbelievers alike—has been a truth that has been consistent with human beings down through history. That very same truth has now come under assault by five justices of the Supreme Court, who were of like mind to change it. This same judicial branch of the government that seems more than willing to alter the definition of marriage also gave us the historic ruling on abortion in the *Roe v. Wade* decision and outlawed the acts of corporate prayer and Bible reading in our public schools.

The Supreme Court has a history of making one terrible mistake after another that has led to societal upheaval and destruction. If we think we can look to them for guidance, we are kidding ourselves. Marriage originated with the God of the Bible, and He is the only one who can accurately define it.

Marriage Isn't Necessary to Have Sex

It is obvious to all but the most naïve that marriage is not necessary for people to engage in sexual relations with one another. No revelation there. Just wake up and look around you. People have sexual relationships all the time without giving the institution of marriage a second's thought.

Civil Unions

It certainly stands to reason that if marriage isn't necessary for heterosexuals to have sex with one another, marriage is also unnecessary for a homosexual couple to engage in sexual activity. In fact, civil unions could have given them the same benefits as marriage. A civil union would have given them all manner of privileges such as property rights, health care, inheritances, and tax benefits, among other things. Civil unions could have afforded appropriate inducements without tampering with the institution of marriage.

Understand this: The only reason that homosexuals desired the right to marry was to water down and ultimately destroy the sanctity of the God-ordained marriage covenant, which keeps society and its families intact. Make no mistake; this is nothing but an attack on godly marriage that will open the floodgates for potential lawsuits, an increased political correctness mind-set, and the ability to control speech in the church. That is what it's for, and it is not about anything else.

Because of this, we have opened ourselves up to a potential silencing of the church. The church will become the focus of lawsuits and maneuverings by the world's system because of a belief founded and established over six thousand years ago, verified and validated by the church over the last two thousand years of human history. Homosexuals did not have to try to change the world's definition of marriage to live the lifestyle they desired. Civil unions could have easily produced it. Homosexual relationships take place every day without marriage.

Homosexual marriage is an attempt to legitimize homosexual behavior. However, no matter how many times you try to legitimize something that God forbids and is contrary to His will, you can never overcome His intrinsic touch that exists down deep in the spirit of every human being. No matter how much you try to overcome something that the Lord has forbidden, the guilt associated with it remains. No matter how hard you try to drown out that still, small voice of God on the inside of you that is telling you what you're doing is wrong, you can't silence the heart. Silence your opponents, yes, but your heart? Never. There is an internal corruption that takes place when we do things we know are wrong.

The same-sex marriage ruling by the Supreme Court is an assault on the biblical definition of marriage and the family, and is in direct defiance of the God of the Bible. Furthermore, it is an attempt to silence the church by passing laws that stop the church from being able to speak. These groups know that if they cannot have what they want, silence the opponent. It is a direct attack on Christianity, your faith, and your freedom to practice it.

Adoption agencies have already had to change some of their policies. Faith-based hospitals and universities have already had to alter some long-standing rules to curtail the possibility of lawsuits. Litigation is already proceeding in the courts to require churches to perform same-sex marriages in their facilities. There is already talk about the clergy being fined, imprisoned, or subject to other legal punishment by the government if they don't conduct same-sex marriage ceremonies. Understand that God is the only one at the end of my life (or the end of the age, whichever comes first) that I have to answer to. I do not have to answer to the Supreme Court, and I do not have to answer to you.

"So, what does all that have to do with the age in which we are living?" you ask.

We're going to explore that in the next chapter. Read on.

21

In the Days of Lot

Luke 17 includes familiar verses that explain what we just read in the previous chapter and how it relates to our current time. Jesus is speaking, but you should frame what He says with the events that are taking place. Sometimes, He refers to historical events, but if you don't understand the history behind what He said, you'll have a hard time understanding what He meant.

Jesus starts a discourse here about the end of the age and signs related to the event:

> Likewise also as it was in the days of Lot; they
> did eat, they drank, they bought, they sold, they
> planted, they builded. (Luke 17:28)

I think it important to say here, to waylay any fear you may have, that our economy will not fail before the coming of the Lord. Notice that the people built things, planted their crops as usual, and bought and sold all kinds of stuff. There may be some dips in the overall financial picture, but our economy will hold up until Jesus comes. There will not be a global economic collapse. You can count on it.

> But the same day that Lot went out of Sodom
> it rained fire and brimstone from heaven, and
> destroyed them all.
>
> Even thus shall it be in the day when the Son of
> man is revealed. (Luke 17:29–30)

To those of you who are anxious and on edge with thoughts of global economic collapsc, takc heart. Let's take a look at these same verses in the Living Bible:

> And the world will be as it was in the days of Lot:
> people went about their daily business—eating
> and drinking, buying and selling, farming and
> building—until the morning Lot left Sodom.
> Then fire and brimstone rained down from
> heaven and destroyed them all.
>
> Yes, it will be "business as usual" right up to the
> hour of my return. (Luke 17:28–30 TLB)

It was business as usual—according to the Living Bible's translation— with eating, drinking, buying, selling, farming, and building going on as always. An economic collapse was never mentioned or even alluded to. Those are the words of Jesus.

His Revelation Is His Appearing

I have said this before, and it is noteworthy to say again: The Revelation of Jesus Christ is what we would call His appearing. When He appears with the church at the second coming, every eye will see Him. Revelation 1:7 says, "Behold, he cometh with clouds; and every eye shall see him."

He comes as dramatically and as quickly as does the lightning from the east to the west. Everyone sees Him. Everyone knows He is here; there are no secrets. However, when He comes for the church at the rapture, He comes as a thief in the night. Not everyone will see Him or behold Him. So there is a big difference between coming for the church and coming with the church.

When the Bible talks about this, it is talking about the Revelation of the Lord, which comes seven years after the catching away of the church. The reason I say that is because these events that Jesus referred to concerning Lot are Tribulation events that come before the Revelation of Jesus Christ, not before the rapture of the church. That is a critical sequence. There is a seven-year time differential from when Jesus comes for the church—when He takes us to heaven, and we experience the Marriage Supper of the Lamb and all the other things that happen there—and when we come back with Him at His Revelation.

Judgment and Redemption

During that seven-year period, there are twenty-one judgments mentioned in the book of Revelation that occur here on earth during the Tribulation. However, the church is not here for that terrible period; it is not appointed unto wrath. Jesus told us that when you begin to see these things happen, lift your head because your redemption is on the way.

> So likewise ye, when ye **see these things** come
> to pass, know ye that the kingdom of God is
> nigh at hand. (Luke 21:31, emphasis added)

So we will see it begin. We will observe the conditions set in motion necessary for these events to take place, but we will not see its completion. Jesus said,

> Even thus shall it be in the day when the Son of
> man is revealed.
>
> In that day, he which shall be upon the
> housetop, and his stuff in the house, let him
> not come down to take it away: and he that is
> in the field, let him likewise not return back.
> (Luke 17:30–31)

That verse is a statement to the Jews, not to the church. It is a statement to the Jews because it happens just before Jesus is revealed. It happens when God is dealing with the nation of Israel. This seven-year period is called the time of Jacob's trouble or Israel's trouble, even though it is a global event. It is also a statement to the Jews, not to the church, just before Jesus is revealed, so you don't need to get all worked up about having enough food to get you through the awful times ahead.

Then God said, "Remember Lot's wife." Now that is a warning that we would be wise not to gloss over.

Abram and Lot

Earlier, we read the scriptures in Luke 17:28-30 that pointed out that just like it was in the days of Lot, it will be the same way when Jesus returns. That is something noteworthy to look at, wouldn't you agree? How was it in the days of Lot, anyway?

Abram and Lot walked together, and both prospered to the point where they finally had to separate. The land could not sustain the two of them. Look in Genesis 13:6:

> And the land was not able to bear them, that they might dwell together: for their substance was great, so that they could not dwell together.

The Living Bible translates the sixth verse like this:

> But the land could not support both Abram and Lot with all their flocks and herds. There were too many animals for the available pasture.

Let's go on to where Abram and Lot separated:

> And Lot lifted up his eyes, and beheld all the plain of Jordan, that it was well watered every where, before the Lord destroyed Sodom and Gomorrah, even as the garden of the Lord, like the land of Egypt, as thou comest unto Zoar.

> Then Lot chose him all the plain of Jordan; and Lot journeyed east: and they separated themselves the one from the other.

> Abram dwelled in the land of Canaan, and Lot dwelled in the cities of the plain, and pitched his tent toward Sodom.
>
> But the men of Sodom were wicked and sinners before the Lord exceedingly. (Genesis 13:10–13)

Lot and Sodom

Lot and the city of Sodom are mentioned as being connected. Scripture says that Lot pitched his tent toward Sodom after he left Abram. The word *toward* is important, meaning that he intentionally aimed his tent flaps in that direction. He could have easily turned the face of his tent away from Sodom, but he decided to face it the other way. In other words, he liked the view.

Scripturally, it is understood that what you associate with, you become; what you listen to, you accept; and what is before you, you begin to embrace. So the word *toward* is important. It means "in the direction of, facing, with respect for, and with regard to something" (Sodom, in this case). That was Lot's first mistake. He had the choice between Sodom and something else. He made his choice.

Lot was very wealthy—God had blessed him immeasurably—so he left Abram and struck out on his own. He did not have to go to Sodom because he needed money or work; he went because he wanted to. So when Jesus said, "As it was in the days of Lot," He's referring to these very things. Going on a little further in this account, we find some interesting things begin to unfold as Lot pitched his tent toward Sodom:

Lot and the Angels

> **And there came two angels to Sodom at even**; and Lot sat in the gate of Sodom: and Lot seeing them rose up to meet them; and he bowed himself with his face toward the ground. (Genesis 19:1, emphasis added)

Angels. That's right, angels. I would guess that some of us have seen or spoken to people we thought were no more than plain, ordinary folks but who were actually angels. The Bible tells us in Hebrews 13:2 that we have possibly entertained angels unknowingly:

> Be not forgetful to entertain strangers: for thereby some have entertained angels unawares.

There are all types of angels, but some of them look just like humans. Some have wings, and some don't. The point is, there are those that look so much like humans that you'd never suspect them of being anything otherwise.

Referring back to the first verse of Genesis 19, we have progressed from Lot aiming his tent flaps toward Sodom to his sitting at Sodom's front gate. Two angels then came to Lot in Sodom:

> And there came two angels to Sodom at even; and Lot sat in the gate of Sodom: and Lot seeing them rose up to meet them; and he bowed himself with his face toward the ground;

> And he said, Behold now, my lords, turn in, I pray you, into your servant's house, and tarry all night, and wash your feet, and ye shall rise up early, and go on your ways. And they said, Nay; but we will abide in the street all night.
>
> And he pressed upon them greatly; and they turned in unto him, and entered into his house; and he made them a feast, and did bake unleavened bread, and they did eat. (Genesis 19:1–3)

I have no way of knowing if Lot was aware those strangers were angels, but he probably did. He probably knew by the revelation of God. But whatever the case may be, he tried to do the right thing by them.

> But before they lay down, the men of the city, even the men of Sodom, compassed the house round, both old and young, all the people from every quarter:
>
> And they called unto Lot, and said unto him, Where are the men which came in to thee this night? bring them out unto us, that we may know them. (Genesis 19:4–5)

"So That We May Know Them"

Let's look at verse 5 again:

> And they called unto Lot, and said unto him, Where are the men which came in to thee this

night? bring them out unto us, that **we may know them**. (Genesis 19:5, emphasis added)

That sounds innocent, but it insinuates something more sinister. The word *know* is significant. Genesis 4:1, talking about Adam and Eve, begins by saying:

And Adam knew Eve his wife.

That verse was talking about a sexual relationship between the two of them. With that in mind, realize that when these men were pursuing the angels, they wanted to know them in a sexual way. That's right. A potential same-sex relationship was what the men of the city were after. Let's replay verse 5 and move on to verses 6 and 7:

> And they called unto Lot, and said unto him, Where are the men which came in to thee this night? bring them out unto us, that we may know them.
>
> And Lot went out at the door unto them, and shut the door after him,
>
> And said, I pray you, brethren, do not so wickedly. (Genesis 19:5–7)

Same-Sex Relationships Are Wicked

The Word of God says that same-sex relationships are wicked. I didn't make that up; I read it directly from the Bible. Furthermore, I just want to go on record as saying that I am in total agreement. "But Pastor King," you may say, "we need to be tolerant." You're exactly right. We should indeed be tolerant— show tolerance with people, not with sin.

Lot tried his best to appease the desires of the men of Sodom, even to the degree of offering them his two virgin daughters instead of the angels. Those of you who, like me, are fathers of daughters, think long and hard about that one. To me, it's unimaginable.

> Behold now, I have two daughters which have not known man; let me, I pray you, bring them out unto you, and do ye to them as is good in your eyes: only unto these men do nothing; for therefore came they under the shadow of my roof.

> And they said, Stand back. And they said again, This one fellow came in to sojourn, and he will needs be a judge: now will we deal worse with thee, than with them. And they pressed sore upon the man, even Lot, and came near to break the door.

> But the men put forth their hand, and pulled Lot into the house to them, and shut to the door. (Genesis 19:8–10)

There are many different interpretations of what this is all about. I know that there are those who say that homosexuality was not Lot's sin, but rather the act of being inhospitable to angels was the culprit. Seriously? Well, this is definitely the ultimate act of inhospitality to angels (or anyone else, for that matter). Nevertheless, I don't think that was what was being discussed here.

You can try to make the Bible say anything you want. However, people who receive from God's Word are those who approach it without prejudice or bias—without an agenda or something to prove. You must let the Bible speak and be willing to listen. You cannot tell it what you want it to say; you only need to do what it says.

> And they smote the men that were at the door of the house with blindness, both small and great: so that they wearied themselves to find the door.
>
> And the men said unto Lot, Hast thou here any besides? son in law, and thy sons, and thy daughters, and whatsoever thou hast in the city, bring them out of this place:
>
> For we will destroy this place, because the cry of them is waxen great before the face of the Lord; and the Lord hath sent us to destroy it. (Genesis 19:11–13)

God sent these angels to destroy Sodom because of the behavior of those who lived there. Jesus said that as it was in the days of Lot, it will be the same way in the day when the Son of man is revealed. Look at it in Luke 17:28, 30:

> Likewise also as it was in the days of Lot; they did eat, they drank, they bought, they sold, they planted, they builded....

> Even thus shall it be in the day when the Son of
> man is revealed.

Remember to put this in the context of the Tribulation period
that is coming, the time when God will judge sin on this planet.
Keep in mind, however, that the signs will come before the
event. Let's go over to Luke 21:28:

> And when these things begin to come to
> pass, then look up, and lift up your heads;
> for your redemption draweth nigh.

If we are not seeing the beginning of our redemption, then I
don't know what we're seeing. It's close. Put this in the context
of "Are we the rapture generation?" God expressed it in Genesis
19:14:

> And Lot went out, and spake unto his sons in
> law, which married his daughters, and said,
> Up, get you out of this place; for the Lord will
> destroy this city. But he seemed as one that
> mocked unto his sons in law.

God was very clear when He spoke to Lot. He said He was
going to deliver him and his family from the incredible evil in
which they had found themselves. He told them to get up off
the couch and get out of town at once. But just before Jesus
spoke of Lot, He mentioned Noah. Let's look what He said
from the New King James Version:

> And as it was in the days of Noah, so it will be
> also in the days of the Son of Man. (Luke 17:26
> NKJV)

The Ark Floated above the Judgment

Deliverance from the judgment was God's plan for Noah. The Ark was his salvation as it floated safely above the water. When the water destroyed everything below him, Noah and his family remained safe, high and dry, and were delivered from the judgment. God knows how to save those who are His, whether many or few.

Just like Noah's Ark floating safely on the water, Lot's escape from Sodom is another example of deliverance—a type of the rapture of the church. The judgment that fell on Sodom will not fall on His saints. It may be judging some in the church— remember the two churches of Philadelphia and Laodicea, and how God related to each one—but not you and me.

My wife and I were on our way to a restaurant some time back and passed a church with a big sign of the rainbow prominently displayed on its façade. We found that interesting, since the rainbow had become a symbol, an icon, used by homosexuals as a means of identification. That church will have to answer to God for that, but that's between them and the Lord. I'm not the judge, folks; I'm just the reporter. I didn't write it; I just talk about it.

God told the angels to inform Lot and his family to leave their home quickly, because judgment was bearing down on them. The judgment of their city was based on the sinful activity going on there. God judged them for their sins, but the iniquity is what caused it. The angels spoke to Lot:

> And when the morning arose, then the angels hastened Lot, saying, Arise, take thy wife, and

> thy two daughters, which are here; lest thou be consumed in the iniquity of the city. (Genesis 19:15 NLT)

Look at Luke 21:36:

> Watch ye therefore, and pray always, that ye may be accounted worthy to escape all these things that shall come to pass, and to stand before the Son of man.

Because Jesus said it, it stands to reason that in typology, the escape is the biblical type of the rapture of the church. Jesus told us to pray that we would be counted worthy to escape. So just as Lot escapes, the church escapes. We escape judgment by the rapture.

Sodom is the root word of *sodomy* and *sodomite*. If you're not sure of their meaning, look them up in a dictionary; I won't define them any further. The obvious point made here, however, is that the sin was not inadequate hospitality shown to the angels. The reference is very clear. No matter what translation of the Bible you reference, it's all the same.

Remember Lot's Wife

Jesus was resolute when He told us to remember Lot's wife. Lot's wife, walking behind him, looked back at Sodom, and turned into a pillar of salt.

> When they were safely out of the city, one of the angels ordered, "Run for your lives! And don't

> look back or stop anywhere in the valley! Escape
> to the mountains, or you will be swept away!"…
>
> But Lot's wife looked back as she was following
> behind him, and she turned into a pillar of salt.…
>
> Remember Lot's wife. (Luke 17:17, 26, 32)

Some scholars believe that the brimstone—an antiquated word for sulfur—found in that part of the world today is actually the remains of the cities of Sodom and Gomorrah. They believe that both cities were at the south end of what we refer to now as the Dead Sea. The Dead Sea is the saltiest body of water on the earth and contains vast amounts of mineral deposits. When the massive explosion took place that destroyed Sodom, some scholars believe that Lot's wife became a statuesque pillar of salt—completely encased by it. If you believe the literal interpretation of scripture—and you renounce the idea that the pillar of salt idea is just folklore—it works, and works well.

Let's read verses 24 and 25:

> Then the Lord rained upon Sodom and upon
> Gomorrah brimstone and fire from the Lord
> out of heaven;
>
> And he overthrew those cities, and all the
> plain, and all the inhabitants of the cities, and
> that which grew upon the ground. (Genesis
> 19:24–25)

Judgment fell on these people because of the perverse activity they were involved in, and it is no different today. Jesus told us very clearly that many people at the time of His coming would embrace the homosexual lifestyle. Same-sex marriage is a sign of the rapture of the church, a sign that needs to be given the attention it deserves.

The judgment of Sodom is a type of last day judgment—a type of the Tribulation. The deliverance of Lot and his family is a type of the rapture of the church. We have talked about the apostasy of the last days—the total desertion or departure from principles or religion—and we have looked at the differences in the two churches and what they are willing to do to embrace these things. These are important signs that are not incidental and need careful examination.

Revelation 11:8 talks about what is going to be happening during the Tribulation:

> And their dead bodies shall lie in the street of
> the great city, which spiritually is called Sodom
> and Egypt, where also our Lord was crucified.

The city where Jesus was crucified is named Jerusalem and is referred to as a type. One of the things that God is showing us about Jerusalem is that it is referred to as Sodom and as Egypt. Egypt is a type of the world or worldly behavior. Sodom is in direct reference to what we just read. That is important because the book of Revelation is showing us very clearly that the population of the Holy Land will embrace this lifestyle.

Case in point: I traveled to Israel some time back and drove forty-five minutes from Tel Aviv to Jerusalem. The day before I arrived, Tel Aviv was celebrating a gay pride event that included over 180,000 participants. 180,000! In the Holy Land! There is an attempt to make Tel Aviv the number one homosexual city in the Middle East. Knowing that, are we looking at something that we were told was coming? I would think so.

During the Tribulation period, Jerusalem is called Sodom. So there is an embracing of that lifestyle. The open acceptance of the homosexual lifestyle and same-sex marriage is a sign of the end of the age. There is no hatred involved here. We love people, but we are talking about biblical standards that the church has to operate within.

At no time in human history has a rational, thinking people ever allowed people to have complete freedom over their sexual activity. We believe, at least for now, that it is wrong and sinful. For example, it is against the law for an adult to have sexual relations with a child. However, there are many people from different organizations who are leading the charge, trying very hard to change that.

We have always believed, and rightly so, that God made us sexual beings—but we must control it. We cannot allow unrestrained sexual activity in our society. You cannot do anything you want to do, anytime you want to do it, with anyone you want to do it with. Restraint is still the order of the day.

For example, we do not condone or tolerate rape. It is wrong in all its forms. There must be self-control. Every mature thinking person recognizes that it is an aberrant and immoral form of behavior.

There must be restraint within the gay community, as well. You ask, "Can a gay person go to heaven?"

The answer is a resounding yes.

Okay then, "Can a practicing gay person go to heaven?"

Different answer. No.

"Well, that's too harsh," you say.

You must remember that I'm not the author of those words. I am not the one who makes the rules, and since I did not make the rules, I do not have the power to change them.

You say, "That's just harsh and uncaring."

Okay then; let's bring it into the non-gay realm: "Can a heterosexual adulterer go to heaven?"

Yes.

"Can a practicing heterosexual adulterer go to heaven?"

Scripture says no. Remember, the rules did not originate with me. There must be restraint in life, and we have to control and keep our bodies with honor.

22

THE MAN OF SIN

We are talking about the reasons I believe that both you and I are members of the rapture generation. Let's look for a moment at the coming of the Lord and the falling away:

> Let no man deceive you by any means: for that day shall not come, except there come a falling away first, and that man of sin be revealed, the son of perdition;
>
> Who opposeth and exalteth himself above all that is called God, or that is worshipped; so that he as God sitteth in the temple of God, shewing himself that he is God. (2 Thessalonians 2:3–4)

This event is coming during the Tribulation period from the man of sin (or the son of perdition, as he is called here), whom we call the antichrist. The good news is that the church will be in heaven and not here for this terrible event. I keep emphasizing this because people seem confused. We will not see this take place because we will be long gone. In fact, the absence of the church is what gives license for this to occur. The rapture of the church must happen first.

> For the mystery of iniquity doth already work: only he who now letteth will let, until he be taken out of the way. (2 Thessalonians 2:7)

This man of sin—the son of perdition, the antichrist—has gone into the Temple of God, declaring to the world that he is, in fact, God Almighty. The ultimate blasphemy.

Daniel and Revelation

The book of Daniel is a prophetic book that gives us tremendous insight into the last days. In fact, the book of Daniel is the Old Testament equivalent of the New Testament book of Revelation. They go hand in glove and dovetail nicely. A description of this man of sin is found in Daniel 11:36–39, which talks about some of his characteristics and personality traits.

> And the king shall do according to his will; and he shall exalt himself, and magnify himself above every god, and shall speak marvellous things against the God of gods, and shall prosper till the indignation be accomplished: for that that is determined shall be done.
>
> Neither shall he regard the God of his fathers, nor the desire of women, nor regard any god: for he shall magnify himself above all.

> But in his estate shall he honour the God of forces: and a god whom his fathers knew not shall he honour with gold, and silver, and with precious stones, and pleasant things.

> Thus shall he do in the most strong holds with a strange god, whom he shall acknowledge and increase with glory: and he shall cause them to rule over many, and shall divide the land for gain.

These verses are talking about the antichrist and his various accomplishments during the time of the Tribulation. In the description of this man of sin, we see that not only does he blaspheme God, but he also sits in the Temple and declares himself to be God. He exalts and magnifies himself above every god and says terrible things about the true God of the universe. If that isn't enough, he is also the man who divides the land of Israel for gain. It is easy to see the unmitigated self-importance that drives him. His arrogance toward God is unprecedented.

The Antichrist Is a Homosexual

> Neither shall he regard the God of his fathers, **nor the desire of women.** (Daniel 11:37, emphasis added)

Therefore, according to the Bible, this man of sin—the world's global leader, the antichrist—is a homosexual, which is an extremely significant situation. There must be an acceptance of that lifestyle and a willingness by the world to embrace it. The world must be willing to welcome a homosexual leader.

As the United States goes, so goes the world. We have seen Mexico, Italy, Taiwan, Ireland, and others elect or appoint openly gay leadership. We have seen it repeatedly. This is a global issue, not just a local one. It states in scripture that this is one of the signs that we have to look at just before the sounding of the trumpet and the catching away of the church.

Because the antichrist is a homosexual, it is necessary for the gay movement to be intact before this man of sin can come to power and take his place in the last day's scenario. This has to take place before the coming of the Lord.

> And when these things begin to come to pass,
> then look up, and lift up your heads; for your
> redemption draweth nigh. (Luke 21:28)

Society and much of the church will accept and embrace gay marriage and the homosexual lifestyle because prophecy declared that it would. Jesus said this was coming and told us emphatically that when we started to see these kinds of things happen to look up and pay attention because our salvation and redemption would be right around the corner. We are closer than we have ever been.

Why would the church embrace homosexuality? Jesus was very clear when He said:

> Jesus answered and said unto them, Ye do err,
> not knowing the scriptures, nor the power of
> God. (Matthew 22:29)

People find themselves in error principally because they do not know the Word of God and the extent of His power. That is why it is such an important thing to teach the Bible to the saints.

I'm not here to give you my opinion; I'm here to tell you what the scripture says. You might say, "Well, I don't like your thinking on this issue; it's not politically correct." Sorry about that, but God told me some things very clearly many years ago when He called me into the ministry. He used the book of Jeremiah, chapter 1, as a strategic element in His call on my life:

> Be not afraid of their faces: for I am with thee to deliver thee, saith the Lord. (Jeremiah 1:8)

The Living Bible says it this way:

> And don't be afraid of the people, for I, the Lord, will be with you and see you through.

As a result, because the Lord told me never to fear people, I don't. I decided to take those feelings off the table. I'm not afraid of you or anyone else. I am, without apology, going to tell you what the Bible says, no matter what you might think of me. To do any less would be traitorous to the God who hung on Calvary's cross, shed His blood, and gave His life for me. To give in to the arrogance that is political correctness, I would be a traitor to Him, His Word, and what He stands for. It is not going to happen.

These people are delusional and do not know the truth. On the other hand, I know the truth, and therefore, I'm not going to take up my cause with them. I'm not against anyone and certainly have absolutely no desire to harm them in any way, but I will defend myself against their desire to harm me.

Society—and especially the church—gets into error because it does not know and doesn't care enough about the scriptures. But now you do. You now know that the embracing of the homosexual lifestyle is a significant sign of Christ's return—an important sign of the rapture of the church. Society is blind to the truth.

> But if our gospel be hid, it is hid to them that are lost:

> In whom the god of this world hath blinded the minds of them which believe not, lest the light of the glorious gospel of Christ, who is the image of God, should shine unto them. (2 Corinthians 4:3–4)

People are blind because the god of this world has blinded them. Because of that, we need to pray for revelation, insight, and awakening. The only way out of darkness is to see the truth, but they will never see it if there isn't anyone around to declare it.

The Propaganda Era

We are immersed in the era of propaganda. It began in the 1930s and continues still today, spurred on by the news media. Like a rocket, it blasts out of Hollywood and into our televisions, the internet, and every imaginable media outlet. Everywhere we turn, we are inundated with insane amounts of propaganda. We have turned the door of our tents toward Sodom.

Because we are so delusional concerning our environment, we cannot even recognize truth when it is presented to us. People are blinded to the truth, and they can't see it. The declaration, "Love wins," sounds so right and valid. All you need is love, right? Look at 1 Corinthians 13:6 (NIV):

> Love does not delight in evil but rejoices with
> the truth.

Love never celebrates sin. You can put the label of love on a perverted lifestyle and even ridicule people who believe it is wrong, but you are merely hiding behind some fake love that is concocted and made up. However, true love is there to get you redeemed from a lifestyle that is going to send you to hell in a hurry, and it has the guts to tell you the truth even when it hurts. Furthermore, it offers answers for your life through the blood of Jesus Christ. That is what genuine love is.

How do we expect a person to change or repent if they continually hear that not only is there nothing wrong with their behavior but, moreover, their lifestyle is accepted on a global scale? How can they possibly comprehend the truth, when the church says that their conduct is acceptable? With that in mind, it seems reasonable to assume that we do not understand sin for what it really is. But know this: even amid all this confusion, Jesus has made a way. He has made a provision.

Even though we may love a person addicted to alcohol, we know that alcohol is destructive, and we need to help them gain freedom from it. The same applies to drug addicts. If they continue in their present lifestyle, there are consequences both here and maybe eternally, as well.

There are consequences to behavior. But there is a giant, persuasive, well-funded, media-friendly group that wants to eliminate any notion of consequences of behavior by shutting down the voice that tells them the truth and shows them the eternal impact of what they are facing. Jesus said this is how it would be in the last days.

Notice carefully how the people of Sodom acted. They were militantly homosexual. Remember what the men of the town said to Lot:

> "Stand back!" they shouted. "This fellow came to town as an outsider, and now he's acting like our judge! We'll treat you far worse than those other men!" And they lunged toward Lot to break down the door. (Genesis 19:9 NLT)

Today, there is a militant mind-set concerning the homosexual lifestyle that Jesus said would be a pervading part of the day in which we live. Homosexuality is a sin for sure, but Jesus is the Redeemer, and He came to this earth in the flesh to help people. The problem is that if we call it sin, then we are somehow bigoted, trying to hurt people, and putting undue pressure on them."

After all," people say, "You shouldn't make those people feel guilty."

Of course it makes homosexuals feel guilty, and it should. But it's not me making them feel guilty. I did not write the Bible, and I do not have the power or permission to rewrite it. I am just going to preach it, believe it, and stand for it. We love people and are not against anyone as a person, but we are against their behavior. We care a great deal about people, but we do not embrace or condone their lifestyle.

23

Drug Abuse and the Rapture

Author's Note

Many times when we talk about the signs of the coming of the Lord, we speak of wars, rumors of wars, earthquakes, famines, and other observations of that type. However, in this chapter, I am focusing on some aspects that are a bit different. All these other signs we've talked about up to now are very much real, but sometimes it's difficult to see the forest for the trees.

Sometimes we can look directly at something without even knowing its significance. We have all been guilty of it, but help is on the way. We're going to draw attention to some things that are directly in front of us that are definitive signs that the Lord is coming for His church very soon.

Some people have argued that many of these signs have been observed from as far back as anyone can remember, and yet, the Lord hasn't made an appearance. All of that is certainly true, but until Israel was restored as a nation in 1948, none of it mattered. The nation of Israel had to be in place as a nation first.

I'm going to go out on a limb here and say that all of us know people who have been affected by drug abuse in some way—either directly or indirectly. It is an epidemic of incredible proportions. The next time you go to a movie, to a restaurant, or even to a church service, you can be confident that drugs, in some way, have touched the lives of the majority of people there. In fact, drugs have likely affected our family, friends, co-workers, and neighbors, as well. No one in this nation has escaped the effects of drugs. Some people have been affected by them more directly than others, but everybody has had to deal with it.

Nothing we say in this chapter is in any way intended to spotlight, condemn, or bring harm to anyone dealing with the issue of drug abuse either personally or with someone close to them. Our sole purpose is to underscore what the prophetic scriptures say about issues that are directly in front of us, so we will not miss what is going on in the world today.

How Drug Abuse and the Rapture Relate

> And then shall they see the Son of man coming in a cloud with power and great glory.
>
> And when these things begin to come to pass, then look up, and lift up your heads; for your redemption draweth nigh. (Luke 21:27–28)

We are at an entry point. We are in a season where signs are emerging. No doubt, the trumpet has not sounded, and the Lord has not come, but the Bible says when you see these signs begin, they are signals to us that we are getting close to the coming of the Lord. You ask, "Just how close are we? How far down the road have we gone?" Good question. I'm just not sure how deep we are going to have to bore down into this thing before the Lord says, "Enough," and takes us out of here.

There are two distinct and different elements of the coming of the Lord.

- The first is the rapture of the church when He calls us to Him. We rise to meet Him in the air.
- The second is when He appears. Every eye shall see Him, and every eye shall behold Him, and they are distinctly different.

So when He said when you begin to see these things—these signs—we should understand what the word *begin* means. *Begin* means to commence, to start, to be the first, the first contact with, to enter upon, the starting point, to come into, or originate. Then there is a process that will take it completely through to its completion. Not a generation shall pass. Once it begins, it will all be completed. Let's look at 1 Thessalonians 5:1:

> But of the times and the seasons, brethren, ye have no need that I write unto you.

Apostle Paul is talking to the brothers at Thessalonica. He said that you don't need me to write to you; you should already know this. You shouldn't need any explanation. But he goes on to say,

> For yourselves know perfectly that the day of the Lord so cometh as a thief in the night. (1 Thessalonians 5:2)

That is what we were referencing earlier. That is talking about the rapture of the church. That is the thief in the night.

> For when they **[not you]** shall say, Peace and safety; then sudden destruction cometh upon them **[not upon you, but upon them]**, as travail upon a woman with child; and they shall not escape. But ye, brethren, are not in darkness, that that day should overtake you as a thief. (1 Thessalonians 5:3–4, emphasis added)

He said that they were not in darkness about this. That day has not come. It comes as a thief in the night to some, but it will not be as a thief in the night to them. They will know, and you should also know the scripture that allows you to understand.

> Ye are all the children of light, and the children of the day: we are not of the night, nor of darkness.
>
> Therefore let us not sleep, as do others; but let us watch and be sober.
>
> For they that sleep sleep in the night; and they that be drunken are drunken in the night.
>
> But let us, who are of the day, be sober, putting on the breastplate of faith and love; and for an helmet, the hope of salvation. (1 Thessalonians 5:5–8)

The Lord's coming is as a thief in the night to the world, but He is making us aware of it. A few things in this passage need your attention. It says in verse 3 that that day will come, as it relates to a woman going into childbirth. I have never experienced it, but I have been around it.

The way you understand whether it's the time for the birth to take place has to do with two primary issues: frequency and intensity. It has to do with time, the birth pains, and how close together they are. They will tell you it's time to go, and then you had better well point your car toward the hospital. My wife, Nora, was slow to let me know that it was time, but I was very insistent.

"Get in the car," I urged. "We're going. Get in the car!"

God also gave us frequency and intensity to help us understand the signs of His coming. There have been signs and other things that have happened down through the centuries, and there are still things continuing to happen, but the frequency and the intensity of the events are significant in knowing how close we are.

So He is saying that the closer we get, the more frequent the signs will be, and the bigger they will become. Frequency and intensity are critical to understanding the times in which we live.

There are three compelling concepts we should take care to remember when talking about the signs of the times—three characteristics that need to be active in our lives as the end times close in on us. We must recognize the time we are in and not become complacent. These three habits are key and help keep us knowledgeable and on pace to understand our situation.

In 1 Thessalonians, Apostle Paul tells us not to sleep, to be watchful, and be sober. Let's look at 1 Thessalonians 5:6:

> Therefore let us not sleep, as do others; but let us watch and be sober. (KJV)

Don't Sleep

The word *sleep*, as Paul uses it here, means to fall asleep or drop off to sleep, to become slothful, or to yield to sin and indifference. He is not talking about being physically asleep but rather being spiritually asleep or indifferent. An example would be the following response concerning a pastor's message:

"End times? Does it really matter? Who cares about this stuff anyway? I want him to teach me something important, like how to prosper."

Complacence and indifference are perfect examples of sleeping.

Be Watchful

Another thing Paul told us to do was to be watchful, which means to be vigilant, to collect one's faculties, to rouse from sleep or inactivity, to give strict attention to, or to be cautiously observant. In other words, stay alert and vigilant.

In the military, one of the most important responsibilities soldiers have is guard duty. While on guard duty, their responsibilities include standing watch and keeping on the lookout for suspicious activities going on around them. For example, the soldier would need to notice if people were trying to access places they didn't have permission to enter. On the battlefield, they watched out for the enemy. They would watch over the troops as they slept or as they went about their regular duties, to make sure no harm came to them. They had to be constantly alert, keeping their eyes open and watching for irregular activities that could potentially be a danger to their fellow soldiers.

The worst possible blunder a soldier on guard duty could make was to fall asleep because they were the alarm bell that alerted all the other troops that something potentially dangerous was about to occur. Sleeping on guard duty was inexcusable.

God says that we need to be as alert and watchful as the watchmen on the walls. We watch. We keep our eyes out for the enemy. The Bible says to watch and pray—to be aware of our circumstances, and then pray about what we see. Watch and pray.

Be Sober

Being sober—the third and last element of this list—plays a critical part in reassuring us that the day of Jesus's appearing does not come upon us unaware. The word *sober* carries with it the idea of being calm, collected in spirit, temperate, smart, and clearheaded. It also means to be free from intoxicants—to be able to think soberly and to exercise self-control and restraint. There are any number of ways to think about those words, but there is probably no need to dig down into it and take it to the extreme. Just look at it for what it means. Simply be sober-minded about where you are and what you're seeing.

In 1 Thessalonians 5:8, Apostle Paul tells us,

> But let us, who are of the day, be sober, putting
> on the breastplate of faith and love; and for an
> helmet, the hope of salvation.

The people Paul is talking about right there, "let us, who are of the day, be sober," are none other than you and me. We are children of the day, not children of the night. We are not children of darkness, but children of light.

He tells us to be sober, putting on the breastplate of faith, among other things. The implication is that you cannot put on your armor if you are not sober, and as a result, you have given the devil a shot at you. The devil was able to take a shot at you that he normally would not have had under usual circumstances. Moreover, because you were asleep, not being watchful, and not sober-minded about your condition, he took his shot at you and put it dead center in the ten ring. Bull's-eye.

You do have authority over the devil, but it does you no good unless you exercise it. Just knowing you have authority over him does not stop him from trying to mess with you. You must purposefully exercise the power you have over him.

Jesus told us to be sober and put aside anything that clouds our judgment. Here's what the mother of King Lemuel taught him to do:

> The words of king Lemuel, the prophecy that
> his mother taught him.

What, my son? and what, the son of my womb?
and what, the son of my vows? (Proverbs 31:1–2)

Now understand, this verse is speaking of King Lemuel. With that said, let me interject something before we go forward. The Bible says that you are a king and a priest unto God. You are of kingly heritage once you made Jesus Christ the Lord of your life. If this verse were there to instruct a king, it would be instruction for you too—unless you think you have more in common with a grifter, a fraud, or someone of ill repute.

You need to realize who you are in the eyes of God. But if by chance you do not understand, then you have another problem entirely. However, if you do realize who you are, you need to begin to act like it. These are instructions for kings like you, so act like one.

Give not thy strength unto women, nor thy ways
to that which destroyeth kings. (Proverbs 31:3)

In other words, the Bible is telling us not to do things that will destroy kings. For example, it is not a good idea for kings to drink wine.

It is not for kings, O Lemuel, it is not for kings
to drink wine; nor for princes strong drink:

Lest they drink, and forget the law, and pervert
the judgment of any of the afflicted. (Proverbs
31:4–5)

I can hear it now: "Well, Jesus drank wine." You don't know the whole story. You have such a shortsighted understanding of the word of God that you think that Jesus drank intoxicants—if you believe that, then you are sadly mistaken. Many people have used that example to justify their actions concerning the use of wine or other alcoholic beverages. The truth, however, is something entirely different. In that day, water purification methods were substandard, and people used wine to purify their water. It was not used primarily as an intoxicant.

> It is not for kings, O Lemuel, it is not for kings to drink wine; nor for princes strong drink:
>
> Lest they drink, and forget the law, and pervert the judgment of any of the afflicted.
>
> Give strong drink unto him that is ready to perish, and wine unto those that be of heavy hearts.
>
> Let him drink, and forget his poverty, and remember his misery no more.
>
> Open thy mouth for the dumb in the cause of all such as are appointed to destruction.
>
> Open thy mouth, judge righteously, and plead the cause of the poor and needy. (Proverbs 31:4–9)

King Lemuel's mother is saying to her son, "Now listen to me, my son the king, if you really want to be a good king, stay sober. Don't do anything to disrupt your ability to stand in judgment of others or make important decisions. You need to make sure to keep yourself from running headlong into a ditch and lose your position as king."

As a child of God, you do not need to put anything mind-altering in your body, either. You need all your faculties fastened in place, intact and in good shape, without intrusion from any outside substance. This passage is talking specifically about drinking alcohol—which is also considered a drug and is not what I'm focusing on in this chapter—but I don't want to pass up the principle found here. If you really want to justify drinking alcohol, you can. You can pull a verse from one chapter in the Bible and another one from an entirely different chapter, throw them in the middle of the table, and wrap a story around them that tries to validate your principles.

"But I only drink in moderation," you say.

That may be true, but you do not have all the facts. You only know what you think you know, not the whole story.

> Be not among winebibbers; among riotous eaters of flesh:
>
> For the drunkard and the glutton shall come to poverty: and drowsiness shall clothe a man with rags. (Proverbs 23:20–21)

That's fairly clear, don't you think? You would have to try incredibly hard to misunderstand that, but if you get religious enough, you can do it. Let's look at Proverbs 23:34:

> Yea, thou shalt be as he that lieth down in the
> midst of the sea, or as he that lieth upon the top
> of a mast.

Have you ever been there? I have. I remember coming home
from a night that was neck-deep full of serious partying, lying
down on the bed, and trying everything I could think of to keep
that thing from moving from wall to wall, and ceiling to floor. I
did not know an inanimate object like my bed could fly around
like that. Of course, my parents thought I was fellowshipping
with church friends at a Bible study. It was like being on that
boat in Proverbs. Look at what the writer said:

> They have stricken me, shalt thou say, and I was
> not sick; they have beaten me, and I felt it not.
> (Proverbs 23:35a)

Have you ever had to look at your car in the morning to see if
you wrecked it on the way home the night before?

"Oh man," you said to your dad, "I didn't do that. Somebody
must have backed into me and put that dent there."

Right.

You would lie about something else too. Your dad was not nearly
as stupid as you thought. He knew exactly what happened to
your car. Now look at Proverbs 23, the last part of verse 35:

> When shall I awake? I will seek it yet again.

Even though the activities involved in people's lifestyle choices
are damaging or possibly even killing them, they persistently

continue on their destructive path. They are sick when they lie down. They can get physically beaten so severely by someone, they don't even know who did it or where it happened. They have no clue how that baseball-sized knot ended up on their head. And then, to make matters worse, they turn around and do it again the next day. That is an addiction. It is destroying their life, but they won't quit.

The Bible says that we should put aside anything that clouds our judgment or takes away our edge. Eliminate anything that restricts our human faculties—we need all we have. Do not take part in any activity that destroys or distorts reality, and stop any pursuit that could inhibit self-control. We should discontinue participation of anything that makes us more prone to sin, confuses our discernment, or increases our vulnerability. We do not want to be unaware on the day of judgment.

These are reasons why I believe we are the rapture generation.

24

SORCERY AND THE LAST DAYS

The Trumpet Judgments

> And the sixth angel sounded, and I heard a
> voice from the four horns of the golden altar
> which is before God,
>
> Saying to the sixth angel which had the trumpet,
> Loose the four angels which are bound in the
> great river Euphrates. (Revelation 9:13–14)

This is what we refer to as the trumpet judgment. It is the sixth
of the seven trumpet judgments of God.

During the Tribulation, while the church is not here, but after
the rapture of the church, there are twenty-one judgments that
come upon the earth. Seven of those are what we refer to as the
trumpet judgments. That is what is going on right here. The
church is absent during the Tribulation, but it is still affected
by them. But right in the midst of all this,

by these three was the third part of men killed.
(Revelation 9:18a)

I want you to understand the seriousness of this event. This judgment right here causes one-third of the earth's population to die. That is one big boatload of people. According to US Census Bureau data, there are between 7.4 and 7.5 billion people on planet earth. If that judgment happened with today's population, we would be talking about the deaths of roughly 2.5 billion people from that one judgment. However, even though that's coming on the earth, we believers are not subject to any of it. We are not here.

> By these three was the third part of men killed,
> by the fire, and by the smoke, and by the
> brimstone, which issued out of their mouths.
> (Revelation 9:18)

Because fire, smoke, and brimstone are all properties related to explosives and explosions, this is probably a type of nuclear event—although there is really no way of knowing with any certainty. However, a third of the earth's population perishes, so I could not imagine it something as incidental as a bag of firecrackers. No matter what it is, it is a seriously dangerous thing.

No Repenting Going On

> And the rest of the men which were not killed
> by these plagues yet repented not of the works
> of their hands, that they should not worship
> devils, and idols of gold, and silver, and brass,

and stone, and of wood: which neither can see,
nor hear, nor walk. (Revelation 9:20)

Can you believe this? Right in the middle of this massive
judgment on the earth, people refused to alter their behavior
or repent of their actions. They are not going to quit. They are
going to defy God at an unbelievable level in the middle of an
event like this.

> Yet repented not of the works of their hands,
> that they should not worship devils. (Revelation
> 9:20a)

Worship the devil? Who in their right mind would want to
worship the devil? Someone with a sound mind having a
desire to worship the devil just does not work. It would be like
putting mayonnaise in your gas tank and gasoline on your ham
sandwich. I will tell you this: If you are going to refuse to repent
of something, it should at least be something attractive. To me,
worshiping the devil does not seem appealing in the least.

Worship the devil? Seriously? Christians won't even worship
the Lord. Why would people in the world want to worship the
devil when they don't want to worship anything? There must
be more to this than what we see at face value.

> And the rest of the men which were not killed
> by these plagues yet repented not of the works
> of their hands, that they should not worship
> devils, and idols of gold, and silver, and brass,
> and stone, and of wood: which neither can see,
> nor hear, nor walk:

> Neither repented they of their murders, nor of their sorceries, nor of their fornication, nor of their thefts. (Revelation 9:20–21)

Verse 21 gives us insight into verse 20. The word *sorceries* mentioned here is related to worshiping the devil, so there is something in that list right there—murders, sorceries, fornication, or thefts—that becomes attractive enough to make someone willing to worship him.

"But I'm not going to worship the devil," you say.

The problem is that many people who worship him have no idea they are.

Sorcery is an important word. It originates from the Greek word *pharmakeia*, where the word *pharmacy* comes from. It means magic. It has to do with magical arts or magical rites. This type of magic should not be confused with the mainstream variety of someone pulling a rabbit out of a hat. No, this is black magic that delves into the occult—exploring areas of the black arts, using drug-induced touchings or contact into the spirit world.

You say that you don't wallow around in the spirit world because you do nothing more than smoke a little dope. Everything is fine, right? See, that's where you're stupid. You could also say, "I don't care about the devil." There is that stupid thing again. It doesn't matter whether you care about the devil or not; he cares about you.

"Well, I don't bother with the devil; I'm through with him."

There is an issue here, however, as the devil is not through with you. It does not really make a lot of difference what you think. He is in the bothering business.

Remember something about the devil. He has no license to work in your life without your permission—coming through your invitation or as a by-product of your ignorance. You just don't know how to stop him. The Bible says that a lack of knowledge will destroy God's people, so the devil can destroy you because of your ignorance. Here is what Hosea has to say:

> My people are destroyed for lack of knowledge.
> (Hosea 4:6)

There is more than one way to bring the devil into your life: You bring him in by invitation, by ignorance, or by your behavior. You don't have to send him a certified letter. All you have to do is act in ways that allow his entrance. Open the door just a little bit, and he will come right in.

"Well, I didn't know I opened the door," you say.

I know you didn't. That's why I wrote this book.

Again, the word *sorcery* comes from the Greek word *pharmakeia*, which is where we get the word *pharmacy*. It means magician or magic, magic arts, or black magic. It refers to drug-induced highs or drug-induced religious practices that could be referred to as witchcraft or the works of the flesh.

> Now the works of the flesh are manifest, which are these; Adultery, fornication, uncleanness, lasciviousness, Idolatry, witchcraft, hatred,

224

variance, emulations, wrath, strife, seditions, heresies, Envyings, murders, drunkenness, revellings, and such like: of the which I tell you before, as I have also told you in time past, that they which do such things shall not inherit the kingdom of God. (Galatians 5:19–21)

One of the words mentioned in verse 20 is *witchcraft*, which is translated as "sorcery." When you start exploring in that realm, you are window-shopping in places you should stay away from. That is not the only way you can open that door, either. Playing around with Ouija boards, fortune-tellers, or palm readers will do the trick, as well. Remember, we are talking about drug abuse and how it relates to the coming of the Lord.

Sorcery, or witchcraft, is in place, even after the rapture occurs. However, when you see these things begin to happen, you know what is at the door. You do not have to wait until you get to the Tribulation to see these things in effect. All you have to do is watch the news or read the paper to see what is going on in society.

The word *sorcery* also means to "concoct a poison." Well, that's pretty much spot on. Drugs are poison for sure. Going by that premise, it involves people who prepare magical remedies. I don't think it's exclusively that, but they are certainly connected because they are mentioned here in the same verse:

Neither repented they of their murders, nor of their sorceries, nor of their fornication, nor of their thefts. (Revelation 9:21)

Physical versus Spiritual Fornication

Fornication is exactly what you would think it would be: sex outside of marriage, but it is more involved than that. All through scripture, the Bible speaks of spiritual whoredom. There are people who have never committed physical fornication but have committed spiritual fornication on a regular basis. So when you see that word, you have to draw the context from it.

According to the definition, if we were talking about an intrusion into false worship and the drug use connected with it, logic would dictate that the fornication mentioned here is more on the spiritual side rather than the physical. The physical side could be involved, but to me, the defiance of the one true God in favor of a false god—or false worship—is more spiritual than physical. Spiritual fornication illustrated here is the betrayal of God, just as adulterers betray their spouse. Adulterers defy their marriage relationship with their spouse by casting away the covenant that they swore.

But notice that that verse also mentions murders. In the United States, the murder rate with a drug-use component is unbelievable. There are all kinds of shootings here: blatant murders on the street, stealthy contract hits, and drive-by shootings. Compounding the tragedy, innocent children and the elderly are just as susceptible as anyone else.

The infamous Mexican drug lord, El Chapo, according to reliable sources, was said to be personally responsible for an estimated forty thousand deaths. He embarrassed the Mexican government by escaping from three different prisons, the last in plain sight of a closed-circuit camera in his cell. However, he was recaptured on January 8, 2016.

Sorcery is at the core of this issue: demonic worship, murder, fornication, thefts, and defiance of the God of the Bible. Statistics show us that conservatively over 90 percent of all violent crime, robberies, armed robberies, home invasions, and thefts are drug-related. People who are involved in this type of activity either have a great need to support their habit or have killed off so many brain cells they don't know what they're doing. Prisons are full of people who have committed violent crimes while in a drug-induced stupor.

The Creosote Pole

Let me tell you something about drug users. They are not just stupid while they're under the influence. Drugs have a lasting chemical effect on the brain that lingers long after the person stops using them. For example, here's an actual conversation I had with an individual some time back:

> "Hey man," the guy said. "Wow, listen to this! I mean, I saw a creosote pole float up on the beach right there."

> "You saw a what?"

> "A creosote pole," he said. "Yeah, there was this creosote pole that just floated up, just come right up out of the water. I made a canopy right here on the beach out of that creosote pole."

> "Really?" I questioned.

> "Really!" he exclaimed.

"Well, that's heavy," I chuckled.

That was one deep conversation with an incredibly rational person, don't you think? Do you think that this guy's voicemail was overflowing with calls from Fortune 500 companies clamoring for his services as creosote pole director? What about it? He should make his case even stronger by getting a tattoo of that thing on his forehead before the interview. I'm sure the human resources department will be duly impressed by his creativity and initiative. The Bible says not to make marks on yourself, but if you are not sober-minded, you don't care about that, either.

I have heard it said, "Well, we're into church growth here. We have to be politically correct, or we'll run people off."

No, we don't have to be politically correct. We need to be biblically correct and truthful. I care about you and the decisions you make. I care that you make decisions in your life that are wise and intelligent rather than dumb and stupid—decisions that will enhance rather than destroy your future.

"Well, that company will just have to take me as I am," Creosote Pole Guy said.

Really? Sorry to be the one to tell you this, but they are under no obligation to hire you the way you are.

"Well, I've been on several job interviews, and no one has said anything about my tats. They don't care if I'm inked up all over."

"How many callbacks have you had for second interviews?"

"Like, none."

Shocking.

That company will not tell you that they care. They would not even tell you if they did care. They just won't call you back.

People are stubborn and rebellious and refuse to deal with the issue, because it had to do with an addiction that they refused to quit. I also believe that all these other behaviors (worshiping the devil, murder, theft, and fornication) were all triggered by their willingness to give themselves over to something that altered their consciousness and resulted in the loss of inhibition. And as we saw earlier, when a third of the population is destroyed, and people still won't repent, they have to be in some extreme stupor. You have to be if you can't see that. But it certainly shows their obstinance.

Let's look again at Proverbs 23:35 (emphasis added):

> They have stricken me, shalt thou say, and I was not sick; they have beaten me, and I felt it not: **when shall I awake? I will seek it yet again.**

The addicts mentioned back in Proverbs had it rough. You know you need help when these terrible things happen to you, and the first thing on your mind the next day is to do it all again. That is an addict. At that point, all rationale goes out the window.

That drug use was attached to satanic worship. The act of communicating with the devil, or communication with the spirit world—to gain some enlightenment from a source other than God—created an altered reality that comes through drug-induced behavior. That is what we are dealing with in society. Sobering, isn't it?

Let me tell you how to stop it. You never start it. You will not have an issue with it if you never do it. This is a serious matter, and it needs to be addressed.

> And in the second year of the reign of Nebuchadnezzar Nebuchadnezzar dreamed dreams, wherewith his spirit was troubled, and his sleep brake from him.
>
> Then the king commanded to call the magicians, and the astrologers, and the sorcerers, and the Chaldeans, for to show the king his dreams. So they came and stood before the king. (Daniel 2:1–2)

A dream is something that takes place in the subconscious or the superconscious mind, but many times, we are unable to recall the contents. These dreams do not take place at a level where normal thought patterns take place. They reside in the spirit realm.

With that in mind, let's talk a little about these people called magicians, astrologers, and sorcerers. In fact, we talked about magicians and sorcerers as being directly connected to drug use. What I want you to notice is their curiosity and involvement with the spirit world. It is linked directly to sorcery, or as we read in the book of Revelation, the use of drugs and drug-induced worship, or drug-induced spiritual enlightenment. Many rock-and-roll groups and other creative people try to enhance their creativity by utilizing the mind-altering effects of drugs. It's a chemically induced trip into another world. Drug use always connects to the spirit realm.

In Daniel 2:27–28, we find magicians, astrologers, sorcerers, and Chaldeans. A Chaldean was known in that day as a professional astrologer.

> Daniel answered in the presence of the king, and said, The secret which the king hath demanded cannot the wise men, the astrologers, the magicians, the soothsayers, show unto the king;
>
> But there is a God in heaven that revealeth secrets, and maketh known to the king Nebuchadnezzar what shall be in the latter days. Thy dream, and the visions of thy head upon thy bed, are these.

In other words, this realm taps into God. The reason sorcery is so abominable to God is that we are seeking out another spiritual source other than Him for guidance. Ultimately, it puts God beneath the source of that information. That is why it is considered devil worship.

You'll rarely see people standing around chanting, "Hail, Satan." They are much too smart for that. However, what they do not understand is that they are entering into a world that starts gaining power over them, and they lose all control. They are in the world of the magicians, the soothsayers, and the sorcerers. They are in the world of the spirit, and it is abominable to God.

Saul was removed from being king because of his trips to the soothsayers. He lost his kingdom because he chose the way of witchcraft over the way of prayer. You have one spiritual guide, and it is the God of the Bible, and not anyone or anything else.

"Well, I'm not seeking guidance."

You might not know what you are looking for, but your ignorance is your vulnerability. Daniel said that these so-called wise men, sorcerers, astrologers, and soothsayers cannot give you what God can give you. God in heaven can do it, but they cannot. That is why witchcraft, sorcery, and drug use are so wrong. A person is seeking direction from someone or something they place in a more prominent position than God holds in their life.

God said that the people had gone "a whoring" when they went to the wizards, sorcerers, and the way of witchcraft. God defined it; I did not call it that. When we do drugs to get high, we have gone a-whoring.

"Well, I didn't know that."

Well, you know it now. That's spiritual fornication. Look at what Leviticus 20:6–7 says about it:

> And the soul that turneth after such as have familiar spirits, and after wizards, to go a whoring after them, I will even set my face against that soul, and will cut him off from among his people.
>
> Sanctify yourselves therefore, and be ye holy: for I am the LORD your God.

God is saying that this is an unholy practice, and you have to be sober and watchful and, by all means, awake. You have to live in a holy way if you want to hear from God. You cannot get to God in any other way. We now have found ourselves living in a world of mindless tolerance. But folks, familiar spirits, wizards, and the like are serious business.

Author Dean T. Olson wrote these words in an article published in the Rapture Forums (www.Raptureforums.com), entitled "Drug Use and the End Time." I believe that it is important, and I would like to share it with you:

> Few drug users know that drug use is tied to occultism. It falls in line with other occult practices designed to prepare the mind for the penetration of demons. The word, witchcraft, in the following verse is translated from the Greek word "Pharmakeia", the root of modern words such as pharmacy and pharmaceuticals. In Greek, Pharmakeia means witchcraft, the occult, sorcery, illicit drugs and magical incantations with drugs and mind control through drug use and drug potions.
>
> Many drug abusers seek the mind-altering euphoria that illicit drugs induce. The Bible strongly denounces these practices because they are part of Satan's strategy to lead us astray. Satan uses drug abuse to change the abuser's perspective of reality. In the 1960's—the beginning of America's insatiable desire for mind-altering substances—the drug-altered reality was called a "mind trip." In the Bible, it

is called 'sorcery.' It prepares the abuser's mind for the penetration of demonic thoughts that separate the abuser from God. When abused long enough, or with the right drug, addiction occurs and Satan is one step closer to his goal of winning the abuser's soul.

The high rate of suicide among the drug-addicted underscores Satan's effectiveness in using drugs to entice man away from God. Satan's goal has always been to wrest souls from God to his dark side. He wins a soul whenever he can convince one of God's Creation to destroy themselves via suicide. And even if the drug addiction doesn't lead to suicide, the need to feed an addiction to stave off psycho-physical withdrawal and attain that euphoric mental state becomes the first priority in the addict's life. As Satan intended, addiction shoves aside friends, family, job, God and even health in the chronic desire to feed the addiction.

There is another sign that we find in Paul's writings to Timothy. He gives us this list of signs of the latter days. One of the signs that he gives us is that people would be without natural affection. I could name lots of people who fit into that category.

Not long ago, I was talking to a beautiful young woman, raised in a Christian home and educated in a Christian school. Her mother told me that she had developed some serious problems and asked if I would talk to her. On the day of our appointment, she came into my office and sat down, and we began the process.

This young woman was unmarried, pregnant, and dealing with a severe drug problem.

This young woman, from all outward appearances, was the epitome of everything nice, wholesome, and good. The problem was, she could barely speak. She could no longer comprehend much of anything or even speak coherently because drug abuse had severely affected her brain. In fact, at our meeting, she was only then coming to the realization that she was pregnant—pregnant with a child who was possibly addicted, as well. She had finally decided to get clean, but she could not even talk to me in a cogent manner because drugs had taken such a toll on her life.

Taking the story down the road a little further, she ended up marrying the father of the child, but without a happy outcome. The child's father also abused drugs, and both of them ended up in jail because of their addiction. The girl's mother is now raising the child. Grandmothers raising grandchildren.

That is a perfect example of the phrase "without natural affection." When you love your drug habit more than you love your children—your flesh and blood—you are without natural affection. When you put the future of your children in the hands of grandparents, other family members, or even state institutions, or when you can't raise your children because of an insatiable appetite for drugs, you have a severe problem that needs immediate attention.

I'm not going to discuss it at length here, but abortion would be another prime example of unnatural affection.

25

TWO TYPES OF DRUG USE

I believe drugs are unquestionably responsible for the absolute disintegration of the sacredness of human life in our society. That is, unfortunately, the world in which we find ourselves.

Legal versus Illegal Drugs

Drug use comes in a variety of forms, both legal and illegal, and at least one can be categorized as both. For example, marijuana can now be considered either way. In most states, the use of recreational marijuana is illegal, while the use of doctor-prescribed marijuana is legal. However, over the past few years, a few states—Colorado, for example—have legalized its use across the board. For you advocates of legalization, I say that if you do not like what the law says, just change the law. If you do not want to live by it, change it.

Then there are illegal drugs: heroin, cocaine, crack cocaine, methamphetamine, LSD, and many others. The list seems to be endless, so I won't even attempt to go down that road.

There are also the legal drugs like prescription medications, painkillers, and mood-altering drugs. You need amphetamines to help get your heart pumping and get you started, and then the barbiturates to help relax you and bring you off the high you're on. You need something to help you sleep. You need something to wake you up. Then, at some point, when those drugs aren't working as quickly as you want them to, you'll start shooting them in your veins.

To compound matters, your tolerance for these chemicals will change over time according to how often you use them. To get the same high you experienced the first time you took a drug, you are going to have to take increasingly larger amounts. It is a never-ending cycle: The more you use, the more you need; the more you need, the more you use. The carousel will continue until your life and health are in serious jeopardy.

People don't set out to become addicts. In fact, they start quite innocently. People who have surgery or were involved in an accident—car crash, sports injury, or an accident at work—often become dependent on painkillers prescribed by a doctor. There is absolutely nothing wrong with being under a physician's supervision for painkillers, but you need to know that some drugs, particularly the opioids—oxycontin, oxycodone, oxymorphone, hydrocodone, and others—are extremely addictive. If you take these medications, the faster you can get off them, the better off you will be.

Remember to be sober and vigilant. Your adversary, the devil, goes around acting like a roaring lion, seeking whom he may devour, so you need to be sober and in touch with reality.

I've taken pain medications for various reasons, but I wonder whatever happened to Extra-Strength Tylenol doing the trick? Do we legitimately need painkillers that are so incredibly intense and addictive? Could it be nothing more than another profit center for drug companies and the medical community? Somebody, somewhere, desires to make a big truckload of money off someone. But I cannot emphasize this enough: The side effects of these drugs are as devastating as the addiction. The quicker you can stop taking them, the better.

Gateway Drugs

We know for sure that marijuana and prescription drugs are both gateway drugs. There is not one person who became addicted to heroin who did not at first fool around with marijuana or prescription medications. Nobody. Methamphetamines are not where the journey begins. People would be horrified to think that they could ever become meth addicts, but they get deceived, play around with a little bit here and a pinch there, and as someone once said, "He who hangeth around creek banks eventually falleth in."

When you play around with these recreational drugs—which are gateway drugs—you are hanging out in the devil's territory. Moreover, the devil is smarter and stronger than you are, especially while you are using these substances. You are certainly strong in Jesus's name, but you do not have His name now—not when you are voluntarily living in the devil's territory. Do not try to pull the name of Jesus out of your back pocket; it's not going to work. It's not going to do you one ounce of good. You have already stepped over the edge. You are playing with a blazing fire that will kill you. It will not only kill you, it will do much worse than that. It will send you somewhere for eternity that I promise you, you do not want to go.

Over 90 percent of violent crimes in some way originate with drug use. Prisons are full of murderers, rapists, thieves, and thugs of all types who got there in some way because of drugs. All gang-related activity has its roots in drug activity—all of it. That is how they make their money.

According to Worldometers (www.worldometers.info/drugs), the illegal drug business brings in approximately $400 billion per year in global revenue. However, these are considered conservative numbers; Drug War Distortions (http://www.drugwardistortions.org/distortion19.htm) sees the figure at somewhere around $500 billion.

Because of drugs, people die prematurely, parents abandon their children, lives and marriages are destroyed, and homes and property are lost, as is all sense of purpose. Previously intelligent people lose their dreams, their vision for the future, and their intellect. Homelessness, in the vast majority of cases, is related to substance abuse.

"Well, this is what I want," you say.

Well, it probably is what you want because you gave your mind away. You gave your brain to something else. You think you want it because you are so goofed up in the head that you don't have a clue what you want.

Paul said in 1 Corinthians 6:12 (NLT),

> You say, "I am allowed to do anything"—but not
> everything is good for you. And even though "I
> am allowed to do anything," I must not become
> a slave to anything.

I even hear people say, "Well, marijuana is just hemp. It's just a plant. I mean, you know, God made plants, right?"

Yes, and He made you too. How did that work out? You're the guy with the creosote pole.

You remember the story in the last chapter of the guy talking about this creosote pole that washed up on the beach? This guy was a surfer in Southern California, but we had this conversation in Knoxville when he was visiting his family, who lived in my neighborhood. We were out walking in the subdivision when we had this conversation, and it was strange, to say the least.

He said, "Out of nowhere there was this creosote pole, and you can't get that anymore. It's like, I believe it was God, man. And we made an umbrella out of it so we could hang out on the beach and cook and surf and stuff." He was totally into it. It was his purpose in life.

He was an intelligent young man, visiting his parents, who were both physicians. He has the DNA of two physicians, but he is into nothing but that creosote pole. All purpose in his life was gone in favor of that pole.

That is a stark reality that's hard to believe. It sounds humorous, but folks, who would have thought that Cheech and Chong, the comedy duo, were closer to reality than we imagined?

"Hey dude, I got a dream from God. It was a creosote pole coming out of the water, man. Just look at that. Wow, dude! A creosote pole. That's heavy, man."

You are really going somewhere, aren't you? You are really going to use your life for the purpose and the glory of God, aren't you? I can tell that you are going to use that fabulous brain God gave you for some great things. No, what you are going to do is destroy so many brain cells that we are not going to know what your personality is or even who you are.

I was talking to one of my preacher friends the other day, and he was telling me that he had taken a lot of drugs back before he came to the Lord. He later turned his life around, and God called him into the ministry. Although the man is a preacher today, he is still dealing with the consequences of the drug use in his past.

He told me, "You know, Pastor Ed, my mind got so messed up doing drugs that in one way it's kind of good—not that my mind got messed up—but that I get to enjoy scripture a second and third time around because I forgot I ever knew it in the first place. So, I get to learn it again.

"For most people," he continued, "they can build on what they have learned, but for me, it's like learning it for the very first time. But I knew it years ago. My mind will no longer work like yours works."

He is a Christian, loves God, and preaches the gospel, but his mind will not operate as it was initially designed to work. Those are his words, his confession, not mine. "My mind doesn't work like yours," he said. Although saved and no doubt going to heaven, he nonetheless hurt himself, and he is paying the price for his actions still today.

Paul said this in 1 Corinthians 6:12:

> All things are lawful unto me, but all things are not expedient: all things are lawful for me, but I will not be brought under the power of any.

The New Living Translation says this:

> You say, "I am allowed to do anything"—but not everything is good for you. And even though "I am allowed to do anything," I must not become a slave to anything.

Paul said not to be bound by anything. I don't care what it is: alcohol, marijuana, heroin, meth; you cannot be bound by anything. You have to be sober and vigilant. Your adversary is the devil. This is the time we live in. Witchcraft is a work of the devil. Here's what Galatians 5:19–21 (emphasis added) says:

> Now the works of the flesh are manifest, which are these; Adultery, fornication, uncleanness, lasciviousness,
>
> Idolatry, **witchcraft**, hatred, variance, emulations, wrath, strife, seditions, heresies, Envyings, murders, drunkenness, revellings, and such like: of the which I tell you before, as I have also told you in time past, that they which do such things shall not inherit the kingdom of God.

Simon the Sorcerer

Let's look at the story of Simon, the Sorcerer, in Acts 8:9–24:

> But there was a certain man, called Simon, which beforetime in the same city used sorcery, and bewitched the people of Samaria, giving out that himself was some great one:
>
> To whom they all gave heed, from the least to the greatest, saying, This man is the great power of God.
>
> And to him they had regard, because that of long time he had bewitched them with sorceries.
>
> But when they believed Philip preaching the things concerning the kingdom of God, and the name of Jesus Christ, they were baptized, both men and women.
>
> Then Simon himself believed also: and when he was baptized, he continued with Philip, and wondered, beholding the miracles and signs which were done.
>
> Now when the apostles which were at Jerusalem heard that Samaria had received the word of God, they sent unto them Peter and John:
>
> Who, when they were come down, prayed for them, that they might receive the Holy Ghost:

(For as yet he was fallen upon none of them: only they were baptized in the name of the Lord Jesus.)

Then laid they their hands on them, and they received the Holy Ghost.

And when Simon saw that through laying on of the apostles' hands the Holy Ghost was given, he offered them money,

Saying, Give me also this power, that on whomsoever I lay hands, he may receive the Holy Ghost.

But Peter said unto him, Thy money perish with thee, because thou hast thought that the gift of God may be purchased with money.

Thou hast neither part nor lot in this matter: for thy heart is not right in the sight of God.

Repent therefore of this thy wickedness, and pray God, if perhaps the thought of thine heart may be forgiven thee.

For I perceive that thou art in the gall of bitterness, and in the bond of iniquity.

Then answered Simon, and said, Pray ye to the Lord for me, that none of these things which ye have spoken come upon me.

When Simon the sorcerer came to the Lord, he had done much in the community, amazing the people with his magic. The truth was, he had deceived the people, and as a result, some even looked at him as the Messiah. However, in the face of a higher power—God's mighty power—Simon the sorcerer turned his life to the Lord and was born again. He repented of what he had done, was saved, and quit the deceptive shenanigans he was involved in. Just like Simon, when you were saved, you repented and stopped doing those things that were contrary to God.

Did Simon the sorcerer use drugs in his deceptions? Well, if sorcery has its roots in drugs, he probably did. But he got saved, and he quit. When you get saved, you quit things. You repent.

This is very important. Do you remember the Babylonian system we discussed back in chapter 9 that will be destroyed? It's an economic way of thinking—Hollywood, news media, finance; it is a system. The Babylonian system is the thing that deceives humankind. That's the whole deal. This is talking about the destruction of that system:

> And the light of a candle shall shine no more at all in thee; and the voice of the bridegroom and of the bride shall be heard no more at all in thee: for thy merchants were the great men of the earth; for **by thy sorceries were all nations deceived.** (Revelation 18:23, emphasis added)

As you can see, one of the great deceptions that indicate the soon coming of Jesus Christ is the deception that has descended on humanity through drug abuse. It is up close and personal, and it is affecting people close to us on every side.

I imagine that the vast majority of those of you reading these words have been affected, in one form or another, by its use. If you are hanging with friends who are messing around with this stuff, get away from them. They are not your true friends. If you are dabbling in it, thinking that God is okay with it, stop. God does not approve at all.

Drugs do some things very well. They will introduce you to a new world—a demonic environment where you are ill-equipped to function. It opens you to something that you cannot handle.

Drug use becomes the thing that keeps us from seeing reality. We must remain aware. We must be ready. We must be alert and forward-looking, just as a sentry would.

26

THE SURVEILLANCE SOCIETY

This chapter discusses how we are monitored both covertly and overtly at some level every day. Surveillance of some type is the way of life in today's society. No matter how knowledgeable you are concerning this subject, I'm confident that the information I'm going to share with you will be quite informative. On the other hand, if you have never researched this world, you are in for quite a shock. That said, I am sure most of you have at least a general awareness of the types of personal surveillance that surround you.

I first spoke about this subject a few years ago. While looking back over those manuscripts, I recollected that most people were shocked by the information I presented. Nevertheless, those things I shared were validated a short time later, as some high-level government whistleblowers pulled the cover off some previously well-hidden activities. Although I knew what I was saying was correct, sometimes a confirming word presented through the national media becomes a corroborating witness to the signs of the end times.

Big Brother: Society under Scrutiny

In 1943, George Orwell began writing what would soon become a wildly popular book entitled *1984*. Published in 1949, one of the characters in that book was Big Brother. Although the year 1984 is now in our rearview mirror, not only have the ideas and concepts that Orwell envisioned happened, but much more besides. The book is still a classic today.

When George Orwell coined the phrase "Big Brother," he had no idea that it would become an integral part of everyday speech. Big Brother primarily refers to some entity such as the government or a higher power that can put all of society under surveillance all day, every day. We are currently living our lives being observed by an overly intrusive Big Brother, who many people agree is the National Security Agency (NSA). The NSA is where most all the monitoring and scrutiny takes place. There are ways to disconnect yourself from this overwhelming examination—by living in a private, secure, out-of-the-way place and getting off the grid—but those places are scarce, if not nonexistent.

How Does This Relate to the End Times?

Now to show you how that fits prophetic scripture, let's look at Revelation 6:1–2:

> And I saw when the Lamb opened one of the seals, and I heard, as it were the noise of thunder, one of the four beasts saying, Come and see.

> And I saw, and behold a white horse: and he
> that sat on him had a bow; and a crown was
> given unto him: and he went forth conquering,
> and to conquer.

The white horse and its rider is the first seal of the twenty-one
judgments opened and meted out on the earth after the rapture
takes place. We're not here.

In Revelation 5, it says that the church is in heaven before the
throne of God, saying, "Who is worthy to take the book and
to open the seals thereof?"

> And I saw in the right hand of him that sat on
> the throne a book written within and on the
> backside, sealed with seven seals.
>
> And I saw a strong angel proclaiming with a
> loud voice, Who is worthy to open the book,
> and to loose the seals thereof?
>
> And no man in heaven, nor in earth, neither
> under the earth, was able to open the book,
> neither to look thereon.
>
> And I wept much, because no man was found
> worthy to open and to read the book, neither to
> look thereon.
>
> And one of the elders saith unto me, Weep not:
> behold, the Lion of the tribe of Judah, the Root
> of David, hath prevailed to open the book, and

to loose the seven seals thereof. (Revelation 5:1–5)

There was only one man found worthy to open the book and loose the seals: the Lamb of God. He opens the seals, and the first judgment is meted out. This is a reference to the man of sin, who is also called the antichrist, the little horn, the king, the son of perdition, the wicked one, and the beast. As you can plainly see, he is called any number of names.

This person attempts to set up global control during this period we call the Tribulation. The good news is that he does not succeed. We learn a little more about this particular person in chapter 13. This is where our focus should be:

> And I stood upon the sand of the sea, and saw a beast rise up out of the sea, having seven heads and ten horns, and upon his horns ten crowns, and upon his heads the name of blasphemy. (Revelation 13:1a)

This beast is the same person we saw in chapter 6 in verses 1 and 2—the man of sin or the antichrist:

> And I saw when the Lamb opened one of the seals, and I heard, as it were the noise of thunder, one of the four beasts saying, Come and see.

> And I saw, and behold a white horse: and he that sat on him had a bow; and a crown was given unto him: and he went forth conquering, and to conquer. (Revelation 6:1–2)

In this passage, he is called the beast. Looking on down in the chapter, we find the second beast in Revelation 1:11:

> And I beheld another beast coming up out of the earth; and he had two horns like a lamb, and he spake as a dragon.

This second beast, a religious leader, is often referred to as the false prophet. Thus, there are two beasts: the antichrist and the false prophet. Speaking of the false prophet:

> And he causeth all, both small and great, rich and poor, free and bond, to receive a mark in their right hand, or in their foreheads. (Revelation 13:16)

The false prophet is a religious leader and creates the desire within the people to receive "the mark of the beast." The antichrist has nothing to do with it. It is the second beast—the false prophet; the religious leader—who does it.

The Rise of Universalism

If words mean anything, the mark probably has some worshipful and religious overtones to it. Furthermore, notice it says that he causes everybody to worship the beast. That tells you that his religion is Universalism, which teaches that all roads lead to Christ. That is why we are inundated with their seemingly endless rhetoric.

I have studied various revivals of the distant and not-too-distant past and found that there was one constant that would inevitably be found where revival had touched an area. Before the revival manifested, one of the themes common to all was the people were convinced that Universalism was the order of the day. In other words, all roads lead to God, no matter how you worshipped or whom you served. Buddha is okay; Mohammed is okay; Confucius is okay; it doesn't matter. If you are sincere and follow your conscience, you will be fine. If you want to get to God, all those roads will ultimately lead you there.

That's hogwash.

There are not ten ways, not twenty, not a hundred ways, or more. There is one way and one way only. The Bible says this in John 14:6:

> Jesus saith unto him, I am the way, the truth, and the life: no man cometh unto the Father, but by me.

"That's not fair!" you cry. You think God's narrow because He only made one way. You ought to be thankful that He even made that one. He could have left us with no way at all, but in His infinite mercy, He did.

27

THE MARK

And that no man might buy or sell, save he that had the mark, or the name of the beast, or the number of his name.

Here is wisdom. Let him that hath understanding count the number of the beast: for it is the number of a man; and his number is Six hundred threescore and six. (Revelation 13:17–18)

We see the infamous group of numbers, 666, quite often. Many times, rock groups hold up a hand gesture that looks similar to the okay sign—putting their thumb and index finger together forming an "O" and the other three fingers sticking straight up. That is the sign of a triple six (666). It has nothing to do with rock and roll. It has everything to do with the occult. It means, "I curse you in Satan's name." It means, "I curse all of you in Satan's name." All the seemingly silly stuff you see people do has a meaning. You do not even know you are caught up in a nasty mess, but you are. It has significance to it, and it is steeped in the occult.

The antichrist uses a mark to try to control commerce, but he falls short of completely pulling it off. There are numbers of people throughout the Tribulation period who do not receive the mark. The antichrist does not gain control of this world, because of Jesus Christ. The King of kings and the Lord of lords, Jesus Christ, and not the antichrist, is the only one who will ever gain control of this planet. Jesus, the Christ, the Almighty God, is the only one who will ever do it.

Nonetheless, the antichrist makes a vigorous attempt to gain control of the world. He has a system that he will use to bring people under his control. It certainly makes sense that if you can't buy or sell without approval or permission, you have to come under some pretty serious scrutiny before that can even take place.

It is also necessary for you to understand that when the antichrist comes on the scene, and this mark is distributed, it will be during the Tribulation period. That means that this mark makes its appearance after the rapture of the church has taken place. So stop worrying if it is something you are going to have to receive or refuse. It would be impossible to get the mark if you are no longer here. If you are in Christ, it is not possible. Nonetheless, the mark is a real thing, and it is coming for a great many people.

The antichrist does not invent the system but adopts and adapts a system already in place to use for his purposes. Doesn't it stand to reason, then, that if you see a system already in place, he may be close behind?

Tattoos

Some societal trends promote playing around with things that are more ominous and serious than people may think. I find it interesting that in our country today, 40 percent of adults have tattoos. What does that have to do with anything? After all, people are aspiring fashionistas and want to be cool and fit in.

With that said, the word *mark* means a scratch, an etching, or a stamp. If you have a tattoo, I promise I am not picking on you. I am just pointing out what I believe are social proclivities, or the craze of the moment, if you will. You may think that fashion is merely fashion and not give a second thought that one seemingly harmless object could be linked to something quite dangerous. I do, however, believe that when society begins to embrace these somewhat ordinary things—such as tattoos—it becomes easier to accept ideas of much greater importance, such as the mark of the beast.

Here's what I mean:

Strong's Concordance says that a mark is a scratch, etching, stamp, or engraving. Thayer's defines it as a stamp imprinted, an imprinted mark, or to brand like a horse, or to carve, or engrave. Kittles Theological Dictionary of the New Testament defines it as a means to engrave, etch, brand, or inscribe. The idea is to put something under the surface, not merely on the surface.

As I said before, the antichrist does not invent this technology, but he will use it for his purposes. The mark will be used for tracking people and all the activities they are involved in, both monetary and otherwise. The insignia of the antichrist will be the numerals 666.

> And when these things begin to come to pass,
> then look up, and lift up your heads; for your
> redemption draweth nigh. (Luke 21:28)

When we see the beginning of these things, look up. We are now seeing the beginning of it.

28

SATELLITE TECHNOLOGY AND THE INTERNET

The antichrist's activity would be severely hampered, however, without the satellite technology that gave us this little thing called the internet. The interconnectivity of the internet is an essential part of this whole process. Keeping track of some seven billion people can only be done using a massive computer network. This process must be in place before the antichrist can implement it for his purposes.

Don't you find it interesting that a battle is being waged to liberate the internet from the control of the United States? The people doing that are not only members of other countries; former President Obama was lobbying for it, as well. There is an overriding agenda at work here. These people know the endgame, even if you do not. You look at this activity in wide-eyed amazement, thinking at a very base level that these people must be crazy. But you would be wrong. There is a government behind the government, with a clear and defined agenda at work, and they know exactly what they are doing. Of that, you can be sure.

Computer-Controlled Cars

Several years ago, Toyota was sued by numerous people claiming that their cars would arbitrarily accelerate for some unknown reason. Drivers would lose control, end up in terrible accidents, and sometimes die as a result. At the time, no one seemed to know what the reason could be. Even though I have no idea what caused it, I am no less concerned that a laptop computer from the other side of the world can now control my car.

Cell Phones

If you think your phone is private and tamperproof, you are sadly mistaken. Your conversations are not your own. That phone can tell the world everything about you. Someone with the knowledge and skillset can access your phone—even while it's charging on your nightstand—turn it on, take control of the camera and microphone, and watch and listen to whatever is going on, anytime they choose.

It is a complete fantasy to believe our communications are private. Edward Snowden showed us that. Remember him? He was the former Central Intelligence Agency employee who in 2013 leaked classified secret information from the National Security Agency.

I find one of his remarks particularly interesting. Before he was interviewed by journalists in Hong Kong, he said the only way the interview would take place was if they put their cell phones in his refrigerator. He knew that privacy would be nonexistent otherwise. It was only then that he revealed how the government was collecting data on its citizens.

Your smartphone has a GPS chip that can show precisely where you are at any given time; it gives away your specific coordinates. The NSA can use that same phone to monitor and record your telephone calls. No one will admit the truth about the recordings, but they exist—all calls are recorded. I'm not saying that every single call is listened to and scrutinized by a team of agents, but they are all digitally recorded—every single call.

Biometric Screening and Facial Recognition

We are all somewhat familiar with biometric screening, but probably not in all the ways it is used. For instance, it is used in the health care industry to track a person's health over a specified period. According to the Centers for Disease Control and Prevention, it tracks height, weight, body mass index, blood pressure, blood cholesterol, blood glucose, and aerobic fitness used as part of a workplace health assessment to benchmark and evaluate changes in employee health status over time.

Another part of the biometric equation is biometric verification or identification. Biometric verification is defined by WhatIs. com as "any means by which a person can be uniquely identified by evaluating one or more distinguishing biological traits. Unique identifiers include fingerprints, hand geometry, earlobe geometry, retina and iris patterns, voice waves, DNA, and signatures."

Biometric screening now uses a great deal of facial recognition. While researching this area, I looked into Great Britain in general, and the city of London in particular. In those areas, video cameras are everywhere. A person can leave home in the morning, drive to work, take the kids to school, go to lunch with friends, shop at Harrods in Knightsbridge, and never be off camera the entire time.

Many of those cameras not only record your image but also hear you. Moreover, if you do something the people monitoring the cameras don't like, the camera can talk back to you. They will let you know you were seen throwing a cigarette butt on the ground and tell you to pick it up. "Hey, you just littered, sir," it says. "Please pick it up and dispose of it properly." Big Brother is watching you. That isn't some futuristic idea. It exists right now.

We are now seeing increasing numbers of cameras being utilized here in the United States. The facial recognition capabilities of these cameras give certain government agencies the ability to run your image through several databases to identify you. They can screen you to acquire information about you. That technology can tell them who you are and where you're from, as well as a wealth of other information.

Remember that these intrusions into our personal lives that we are willing to put up with have their roots in combating terrorism. That is what makes it palatable for us. We become willing to give our freedoms away because we are fearful of what the terrorists may do. Meanwhile, in the name of capturing these radical extremists, the government is looking into everything we do.

In this biometric world we are living in, we are quick to accept facial recognition for reasons of security, surveillance, and scrutiny. It is also done to give you preferential access. It may allow you entry to an area where others aren't permitted to go.

Retinal scans—the process of scanning your eyes—provide a deeper level of security and a greater level of scrutiny.

In addition to these technologies, fingerprinting is still widely used, as it has been for decades. Also, palm prints are also being utilized.

Many airports now utilize prescreening techniques to help move passengers through security areas. If you have been prescreened, you no longer have to go through the process of taking off your shoes, your belt, and all the rest. All you need to do is place your hand or your palm on a digital reader, and you're done. You have to pay a little bit to get it done, but it's well worth it. It makes travel so much simpler. It's worth a little trouble to get it done on the front end, but not having to do all the mind-numbing things the airport makes you do is priceless.

GPS

Now we come to satellite global positioning systems (GPS), a space-based navigation and surveillance system that provides location, time, and other information in all weather conditions. GPS is an incredible technology, especially convenient when it is installed in your automobile. You can enter the address of your destination, and your navigation system will lead you to the exact place you want to go. It is fabulous technology, and if you have it available, you probably use it all the time.

If you don't have a GPS system built into your car, you can easily utilize the one built into many current smartphones. It's really simple. Enter a destination address in a GPS app on your smartphone, and it will do the same thing as the model installed in an automobile. Make it easier on yourself by ordering a simple mount that matches up with your vehicle and your phone. It's now hands-free and safer to use. Those things are very accurate, to within a few feet over thousands of miles. James Bond could only wish he had a phone like yours. I love my GPS. It's a very useful and important part of my life.

GPS is not only used for getting you to your destination; it is also used to collect your personal data. If there is a cell phone or smartphone in your pocket, you are under constant scrutiny. Technicians can determine your location, the places you visited, and the length of your visit. Furthermore, if you went to someplace suspicious, a technician can turn on the camera and microphone and observe what you do and say.

I'm not saying that someone is surveilling you everywhere you go and every time you go there. There are not enough people in the world to monitor everyone to that degree. However, if the computer that is scrutinizing your phone alerts an employee of the monitoring firm that you visited a suspicious place, an alert is given, and your visit will then be analyzed—especially if subversive or flagged words are heard.

The GPS in your phone can tell others your current location, how long you have been there, and how many times you've been there. If you go there every day, it will know. If you go to that same place three times every day, or twice a week, or twice a month, it will know. It acts like your younger sister; it will tell on you.

Tracking Your Automobile

GPS tracking devices can be installed in your car or truck. For instance, if law enforcement suspects that you are engaged in some criminal activity, they can place a tracking device on your automobile. If your Mercedes is parked outside in your driveway, a judge will rule that there is no expectation of privacy, and it can be legally outfitted with a GPS tracker without a warrant. You can be tracked everywhere you go, and the results can be used against you in court.

Email and Text Messages

Your emails and text messages are also monitored and recorded. With that said, it seems odd to me that the only people who can totally lose emails are those with lots of political power. The rest of us cannot seem to get rid of ours on purpose, but certain people in government have an uncanny ability to accidentally and permanently misplace theirs. Is that a little suspicious to you? It is to me. Be careful what you put in your texts because they are monitored and can be forever recoverable, just like email.

Photos

Just like email and text messages, photos have metadata stored in them. Every picture you take with your phone is date and time stamped along with GPS information. If you forward a photo to another person—if you decide to use it on Facebook or another media outlet—the information stays with that photo forever. Additionally, if the person you forwarded it to decides to use it or send it to someone else, your information—the metadata—goes with it. Even though you may not see the information on the photo, it is retrievable. Forever. People who want to know will know where and when you took the picture. Just so you'll know, there are settings that can turn this feature off.

RFID Chips

There are two types of radio-frequency identification (RFID) chips: passive and active. Passive low-power chips rely on an RFID reader to activate them, while active RFID chips use an internal power source and are always active.

An RFID chip is a radio frequency device that can be embedded in many things—a credit card being one. They are not like the old bar code scanners where you had to hold it up and shine the laser on it. RFIDs actually emit a signal.

All your credit card purchases are traceable. Because your credit cards have RFID chips in them, they are not only traceable after you make a purchase; those cards emit a signal and are detectable as you walk in the front door of the store. These chips are even detectable when you pass near any RFID reader, wherever they are located, even at the gas pump at your local service station. You do not even have to slide the card. These readers detect the card and the information contained in it while that VISA or American Express card is still in your pocket. As technology increases and becomes more advanced, everything seems to get smaller.

How strong is the emitter? How far away will a receiver pick up the signal? It depends on the power source. Some of these battery-powered RFID chips are actually activated by movement or heat. In other words, you are the battery. As long as you move, or the card is in relatively close proximity to a heat source, the RFIDs emits a signal and can be read without the worry of the battery ever losing power. Sunlight or artificial lighting activates some of them, so the battery is not going to wear out. How far away you can detect one of those chips depends on two things: the emission strength of the chip and the strength of the receiver (reader).

Not only are your credit cards tracked, but also your purchases made on those cards are recorded, as well. The item purchased, where the purchase was made, and the time of the transaction are all recorded. If they want to find out, people can know all about you.

Detectable by Satellite?

Can RFID chips be detected by satellite? I'm not sure if that's the case, but many scientists certainly anticipate that happening. Once that occurs, information transfer does not need the internet; it will go directly to the satellite.

RFID Is Everywhere

Many of the things you buy have RFID chips in them. These chips could be visible on the product, hidden in the labels, or buried somewhere on or in the item itself. Have you ever wondered why the person at the checkout takes your purchase and runs it over a scanner? There's a tag in there with an RFID chip in it that has to be deactivated so the store's security system won't go off when you walk out the door.

RFIDs are not used just to make the security system go off; they are also designed for inventory control. These chips can tell management how many blue shirts in size large have been sold today, this week, and this month. It tells them how many bags of a particular brand of potato chips have been sold. The software creates and maintains a running inventory as people go through the checkout line or through the exit where that information can be detected.

For instance, magnetic ink is used on many items like soft drink cans. Some magnetic ink can respond to a scanner. Manufacturers have created emitters so small that they are no larger than the size of the dot on the top of the letter "i" in the advertising copy. Amazing.

Let's take this magnetic ink technology a bit further. Some of those RFID chips are not only active in the store, they are also active at your home. The magnetic ink and the information contained in them, along with all of the things related to the product, are still readable long after it leaves the store.

Monitoring Your Trash

The information is even readable from inside a trashcan. If you live in an environmentally conscious area, your garbage cans can be quickly scanned, and you can be fined or arrested for throwing away the wrong kinds of trash. Your punishment would be consistent with how politically correct your part of the world is. If you do not recycle, you can be punished for it, and your trashcan will tell on you.

Trashcan surveillance is not just some nutty notion from Crazyville. Those cans exist in Great Britain and some places in the United States. Government workers can tell what you put in the trash. If you were not a good little boy or girl and put glass in the plastics bin or food in the paper container, these people can come and knock on your door. You think we are under surveillance?

Smart TV

Smart TV is big business and very high-tech. In fact, a well-known television manufacturer warned consumers that if they did not want their private information known, not to say anything of a sensitive nature near some of their televisions. Smart TVs can be controlled by your voice, and because it has to receive voice commands from you to respond, it records and remembers your voiceprint.

There are also cameras in the smart TVs used by market researchers that see how you react to a product's advertisement. If you respond favorably, they will send other commercials of similar products to you.

Isn't it interesting that if we make an online purchase of underwear and socks, that for the next few days, we are going to be inundated with underwear and sock advertising from every internet retailer out there. The entire sidebar has nothing but ads for boxer shorts and athletic socks. It's a little creepy that somebody actually cares what size and type of underwear I wear.

Marketers are extremely sophisticated and know what we have purchased, and they begin to target us in a specific, unique way. That really isn't bothersome as much as it's troubling that marketers know me at that level and have that kind of personal data. It is kind of funny, but that's where we are.

Think about it. There are cameras, microphones, and smart televisions everywhere connected to the internet, and because of that relationship, they can be hacked. Somebody may be looking at you while you are watching television in your bedroom.

Cable Boxes

Cable boxes have been found to have cameras in them. After disassembling their boxes, people have discovered the cameras. I don't know if they all have cameras in them, but some do. These cable boxes can take a real-time digital video of people sitting in front of their televisions. Intrusive? You bet it is.

Game Consoles

Game consoles like the Xbox, Nintendo, Wii, and the Sony Playstation all come with the ability to connect to the internet. To be able to play certain games on the web, microphones and cameras are also required. These things are sophisticated detection devices in your home. Think about it. If a cell phone can be turned off or on at the will of the hacker, don't you think these devices can be controlled the same way? These devices do not have to be turned on or in use for hackers to infiltrate them.

Baby Monitors

Baby monitors can be hacked, and people are using them to observe children in their cribs. Criminals are also using these things to see if anyone is at home. These guys can tell if it is safe to enter your home and steal your stuff.

Security Cameras

Security cameras installed in your home or business are all hackable. These cameras can be used by criminals to monitor everything the lens sees.

The upshot of this is that the less time you spend on the internet, the better off you are. Just about everything is hackable. Somebody out there knows how to get around it.

Garage Doors

We have a life chock-full of conveniences. For instance, our smartphones can be used to open and close our garage doors from remote locations. If we leave the house in the morning and forget to shut the thing, just pull up the app on your phone, press the button, and voila—the door closes.

That is truly a great convenience. But there is a downside to it as well. There is a hacker out there somewhere who knows how to raise that garage door and let his criminal friends into your garage. Then you can say goodbye to thousands of dollars' worth of tools, sports equipment, and automobiles. Plus, it is a convenient way to get into the house, undetected. Then the loss can really become substantial.

Door Locks

You may have installed an internet-based, remotely activated door lock on the exterior doors of your home. They are convenient because you can let the repairman in the house without taking off from work to meet him. He calls, you press a button on your smartphone to let him in, and when he finishes, you press another button, and the door locks behind him. Easy.

But remember, the hacker can open your door too, and he is not going to worry about your broken appliances. It is my humble opinion that the less you rely on these technologies, the better off you are.

Internet-Connected Thermostats

There are internet-based thermostats available that control your heat and air-conditioning. People can monitor those things to determine if you are a good little environmentalist or if you are an environmentally wasteful person. What if you want your air-conditioning set at 69 degrees year round? Sorry, you waster. The magic number for your HVAC system is 78 degrees in the summer, and 65 degrees in the winter. Enjoy.

Electric Meters

Smart electric meters can be installed in your home that can tell when you turn on your electric toothbrush or your hairdryer. Guess what: The internet relays that information back to somebody, somewhere. They know when you brush your teeth. Count on it.

Amazon Echo, Google Home, Apple Home Pod

These are quite possibly the ultimate convenience devices. What are the morning headlines? Just ask. They will tell you the time and the weather forecast. They will keep you updated with the daily news and give you a current weather report. They will set a timer or an alarm, play music, and read a book to you. They will create a to-do list, turn your lights on or off, lock the front door, activate your home's alarm system, turn the temperature setting on your thermostat up or down, order a pizza, and tell you a joke. Well, you get the point.

But all this convenience comes at a price. Everything you ask Amazon's version, the Echo, is saved by Amazon. Everything. It knows everything you search for. It is just another way of tracking you.

Are you coming over to my side now? So let me ask this question: Do you think we live in a surveillance-driven society or not? I'll bet you answer yes. Do you understand why the antichrist is so into this whole internet thing? The internet is his tool. The internet is his scheme. The internet is what he is going to use.

Get Off the Grid

There is a place in West Virginia that has the distinction of being the only place in the United States where there is no internet access. There is no satellite scrutiny, whatsoever. Preppers love that place. Do you know what a prepper is? A prepper is someone who is actively preparing for a life of hard times following some future catastrophe. They are actively storing necessities for life such as food, water, seeds, clothes, and weapons.

Preppers consider many things when choosing an area to live their life—climate, temperature, growing seasons, and growing cycles, especially if they need to grow their own food. Security is another issue; population density is important, as well. Many considerations go into why one place is better than another. For a variety of reasons, one of the best places in the country for preppers to locate is on the Cumberland Plateau in the Middle Tennessee area, between Nashville and Knoxville. The area is perfect for their needs. It's a prepper paradise.

Big Brother Is Truly Watching

Going a little further with the surveillance issue, people are now talking about outfitting much of the wilderness areas of the United States with cameras. The reason would be to get ahead of the curve on forest fires and other things. Not only will the populated areas have them, but now the wilderness areas are going to be scrutinized, as well. Even though the cameras aren't necessarily going to be dangling from the trees, we know the capabilities of satellites. They can see through smoke and utilize other pertinent technologies as well. If the government suspects potentially subversive activities are taking place, wilderness or not, they can scrutinize that area by satellite—no helicopters needed.

Need a Roof?

In 2011, we had a major hailstorm in Tennessee that damaged thousands of homes and automobiles. It seemed that everyone you talked to was replacing their roof or getting their cars repaired from massive hail damage. I had to have a new roof put on my house.

When the roofers came to the house and made a presentation on their great products, they already had a complete package of aerial photos of my home. I am not talking about satellite photos, either. I'm talking about low-level images from a variety of angles. The salesman told me that these pictures were available from a company that specializes in that type of product. You have probably noticed the helicopters and small airplanes flying around at low levels close to where you live. Have you ever wondered why that was happening? Among other things, photographs and video of the roofs of the homes in our neighborhoods are probably being recorded. Roofing companies can tell from those images which ones need to be replaced. The next thing you know, a salesman is calling from a roofing company to set up a meeting. Well, there you go.

But as crazy as that sounds, I had no idea that the photos were in such incredible detail. The salesman told me how many squares of roofing I needed, and what the price would be before he even got a ladder off his truck. He had all the necessary information to give me a quote right there in front of him.

This technology surprised me. I knew about Google maps and satellites, but these images were from two hundred feet.

I'm sure you've seen the cars from Google that go up and down the road taking pictures of all the streets, houses, and businesses. You can go online and look right at your front door if you want to. It's not hard. Everybody can do it.

Black Boxes in Cars

Automobiles now have black boxes in them with computers inside. It became federal law that by 2015, all cars had to have these little computers in them.

A black box is a computer that is interrelated to all the car's systems. It alerts the owner if something's wrong or the vehicle needs service. The box will send you a text to tell you your oil needs to be changed or your tire pressure is low. It will also tell you if there is a recall for your car. That technology is quite common today.

My automobile is connected to a satellite that reads the content of the onboard computer in my car and automatically knows its condition. That statement leads me to this question: If people can read the repair record of the car, can they also read my driving record?

Whoops!

I was just reading about a man who was involved in a car accident. When the police officer asked him his side of the story, he said he was driving 65 miles per hour with his seat belt fastened. I guess the guy didn't know about the black box in his car because when the officer checked it out, the little black box told him he was actually driving over 100 miles an hour without his seatbelt fastened. Whoops! The black box told what really happened. That technology is in your car right now.

Hold on, There's More

Some vehicles have autoresponse phone services like OnStar, for example. If an accident happens or you have car trouble, the computer notifies the service automatically, and they call you within seconds.

If your airbag goes off, that little black box will send an automatic signal that will dial 911 for you. The emergency operator will call you first to see if you are able to talk and to see if it was something other than an accident. If you do not answer their call, an emergency vehicle will automatically be sent to your location. Here's another fun fact: if that smartphone in your pocket can be tapped into, then that emergency phone in your car can be hacked into, as well.

So your story is that you were cruising down the highway at exactly 70 miles per hour because that is the posted speed limit. Of course, you, like the rest of us, are unwavering about obeying it and would never consider to push it even a little. But the little people in that tiny black box know the truth. You can't pull the wool over their eyes, no sir. Those tiny people pay close attention to you. They know your exact location and can listen in on your conversations at the same time, if they choose to.

Hackers can also gain access to those little black boxes in your automobile. After they successfully gain access to it, they can even drive your car without your assistance.

Drone Aircraft

Drone pilots can be sitting in their office in Nebraska or Colorado and fly a combat drone through the mountains of Afghanistan. An unmanned combat drone with a full complement of military ordinance—including machine guns and missiles—is being piloted by someone with a joystick, in an air-conditioned office, raining an inferno of misery down on the enemy on the other side of the world.

Drone helicopters are used extensively as well. They are full-sized helicopters with no pilot in them. They can carry a larger payload and stay aloft much longer.

These drones are great, but truthfully, stealth is one of the best ways to collect data. If you do any research on drones, you will find that there are drones the size of mosquitoes—and actually look like mosquitoes—that can go inside houses and offices. These little creatures can covertly go into places where a normal-sized helicopter just cannot go. They fly clandestinely into a bad guy's headquarters and help to usurp their nasty, illegal plans.

The government has already earmarked hundreds of millions of dollars for the development of drone technology. These drones are going to be put in the hands of local law enforcement, as well. If there is a disturbance down here at the intersection of First and Elm or wherever, the sheriff will be able to send a drone to photograph the area even before he dispatches an officer. That's a pretty good use of the technology.

I want you to recognize the age that we are living in. I did not make this stuff up. This time of surveillance was prophesied long ago and is another sign that Jesus is coming soon.

Nothing Is Off-Limits

Every internet-based device is hackable, whether it be a thermostat in your home or an automatic crockpot controlled by your smartphone. Electric meters, security cameras, and even combat drones are no exception.

Not all of this technology is fundamentally bad, however. Technology, in and of itself, is neutral—neither good nor bad. Whether it is harmful or destructive depends on who has control of it.

Be Aware

Whether you are in public or not, you should never assume that you are immune from being surveilled by a camera. If you are outside, err on the side of caution and believe that a camera somewhere is recording your image. Wherever you are, chances are pretty good that your likeness is being documented for all posterity.

29

Assume You Are Being Surveilled

Anytime you are in public, assume someone is watching you. There is no more privacy. Your emails, your phone calls, your posts on Twitter and Facebook, your purchases, your TV viewing habits: Everything is monitored. People know what you watch on TV. They know what channel you watch, how long you watch it, and even when you change the channel. How do you think popularity statistics are gathered by TV shows?

Your personal profile is built from the data they collect. This information is a clear snapshot that tells whoever wants to know all about you.

You Are a Threat

Did you know that you are a threat? In fact, you are a national threat if you show up in the following list.

You'll find that you are a threat

- if you are a committed Christian; Evangelical or Catholic, it doesn't matter. A committed Christian is potentially a threat to the government and in their eyes needs watching. Uncle Sam collects your data, and he knows who you are.
- if you homeschool or send your children to Christian school.
- if you are a gun owner. I am not talking about a criminal, but a person who is a hunter, sportsman, collector, or simply concerned about home protection.
- if you are a member of the NRA or similar organizations.
- if you store up food. You say, "Well, how would the government know if I store food?" Remember, all of your transactions are recorded. If you have a loyalty card at a grocery store, they know it and can access it. All of your purchases and payments are connected. It's in your profile.
- if you are a political conservative.

I'm guilty on all of the above. So send the drone, that's all I know. But unlike the previous list, I'm totally innocent of this one.

- If you are a prepper, you are also on the threat list. You need to understand that people who know how to do it can track your purchases. As a result, they know what you buy, where you bought it, and how much of it you bought.

Health Care

Health care is the number one way to track you. People are going to track you because your resistance to all this stuff will be eliminated when you give up the information for your own physical health.

Many times, people think the mark of the beast is going to be forced on them at gunpoint. That is not the way it is going to be. There will be people lining up voluntarily to get the mark, and some will be excited about it. They will not want to carry a card that can be hacked.

Your health records, financial records, family status, and purchasing history will all be available. Information about where you travel, how long you stay, and what you did there builds a profile about you. And it all starts with your health care records. That is what will open the door to all the rest of it.

A while back, someone told me about a recent visit to the doctor's office. As he was filling out the forms, he came upon the obvious question about gender. Not too long ago, there were only two possible answers: male or female. Not in that doctor's office. No, sir. He said that there were ten or so, some concerning sexual preferences. I wish they'd let me design the forms. I'd add a selection box after every question that said, "None of your stupid business."

There was also a very pertinent health care question in there that asked if he was a gun owner. Seriously? I've been trying to figure out just what being a gun owner has to do with health care. Just so you'll know, I totally disagree with the questions and the right of anyone to ask them—any of them. It makes absolutely no sense whatsoever.

Important Information

The information in this chapter is vitally important because it is seldom included in conversations about the end times. We hear of wars, rumors of wars, earthquakes, and other things quite a bit, but we hear nothing about the information contained here. I'm not dealing with the obvious stuff we hear about all the time. I'm dealing with the information you've missed; the information we have all missed. All of this is designed to show you that Jesus is coming soon, and there is no doubt about it.

All the technology that we have discussed in this chapter is currently in place. As a result, we have been given some important responsibilities, including the following:

1. **Be aware** of what's going on in the world around you, of current events and how they impact the end-times conversation. By taking the time to read this book, you have an advantage. You now have a much better grasp of what's really happening in the world today.
2. **Use your influence**. It's the most powerful tool you have at your disposal. Many Christians have given up and are just biding their time, waiting for the rapture. Well, folks, that is not the answer to anybody's problem. You must use your influence for Jesus Christ. Turn as many people to the Lord as you can. Bring people with you to church. Use the tools available to you for the gospel.

3. **Don't be afraid.** Don't stand around, shaking like a dog in the cold. Don't be afraid; we won't be here for the Tribulation. I don't care what the economists and politicians tell you, the economy is not going to collapse. It is going to remain in place and function as it was designed. The Bible says that when Jesus comes, people will be buying, selling, and conducting business as usual. The economy will go haywire after we leave, but it's not going to happen before we leave this earth. The economy stays in place.

Use what is at your disposal, and don't be afraid. This is our time. God is getting ready to harvest this planet, and you are His instrument. Use your influence for the Kingdom of God and be personally prepared. Trust the Lord. That is all you can do. But that's enough.

I can promise you that I am not afraid. I am not afraid to talk about this so that you can become more aware. I'm going to talk about this on every outlet open to me. It's going on the internet as well as our television show because people need to know.

People need to know that Jesus is coming soon.

We have to be ready.

Books by Dr. Ed King
Please visit poweroftheword.com
Also available on Amazon.com

Will My Pet Be in Heaven?
We love our pets. When they leave us, there is an emptiness that forms inside of us that only they could fill. In this revealing book, you will find comfort and hope. The question will be answered: Will we see our pet again?

Dedicating Your House
Your house plays a significant role in your life. Dedicating it to God holds more spiritual importance than you may realize. God's desire is that we experience His abundant life. So, in dedicating our homes, we are cooperating with His sacred purpose. Dr. Ed King has dedicated his own homes and has received the benefits that come from it. Our homes can be established places of blessing and peace, where we rest and live a harmonious existence with God and our families.

Loyalty: Going Beyond Faithfulness
In order to become effective Christians, we must all develop the character trait of faithfulness, in both our relationship with God and our relationships with our fellow man. However, faithfulness is but entry-level relationship, and God truly desires more from us. As important as faithfulness is, He desires us to be as King David was to Jonathan: loyal!

The Timing of God
In this dynamic book by Dr. Ed King, you will begin your pursuit of the flawless timing of God by discovering the true timetable that God has set up for you at creation. You will see that everything in life has a time and a season.

30 Days to a Better Prayer Life, by Pastor Nora King
In this exciting and insightful book, Nora King brings fresh revelation and practical teaching together to help you experience the release of God's power through prayer. She shares treasures that she's unearthed over years of study and personal devotional time spent with God. You will learn day by day how to improve your prayer life and enter into God's presence through these simple principles. You don't have to struggle in prayer any longer. Take this first step to a better prayer life!

CPSIA information can be obtained
at www.ICGtesting.com
Printed in the USA
BVHW081230130219
540160BV00003B/133/P

9 781973 638872